Navigating ADHD For Adults

12 Proven Strategies and Techniques to Harness your ADHD in Relationships, Work, and at Home

Phoenix J. Waldren

Copyright 2024 - All rights reserved.

All rights reserved. No part of this guide may be reproduced, transmitted, or distributed in any form or by any means without permission in writing from the publisher except in the case of brief quotations embodied in critical articles or reviews

Legal & Disclaimer

The content and information in this book are consistent and truthful, and it has been provided for informational, educational, and business purposes only.

Table of Contents

Introduction **1**

Chapter 1: Mastering Time Management **5**
- ❖ *Visual Time Management Tools for the ADHD Mind* **6**
- ❖ *Breaking Large Projects into Manageable Tasks* **9**
- ❖ *Overcoming Time Blindness with Simple Techniques* **12**
- ❖ *The Pomodoro Technique Adapted for ADHD* **15**

Chapter 2: Organizational Systems That Work **21**
- ❖ *Decluttering Strategies for the Chronically Disorganized* ... **22**
- ❖ *Digital Organization for the ADHD Professional* **25**
- ❖ *Creating an ADHD-Friendly Workspace* **29**
- ❖ *Routine Checklists to Maintain Order* **32**

Chapter 3: Navigating Professional Settings **40**
- ❖ *Strategies for Staying Engaged in Meetings* **41**
- ❖ *Managing Workplace Relationships with ADHD* **44**
- ❖ *Techniques for Effective Professional Communication* **47**
- ❖ *Handling Workplace Distractions* **51**

Chapter 4: Stress and Emotional Regulation **58**
- ❖ *Cognitive Behavioral Techniques for Emotional Control* **63**
- ❖ *Managing Anxiety in High-Stakes Situations* **66**
- ❖ *Using Physical Exercise to Manage Emotional Stress* **70**

Chapter 5: Leveraging ADHD Strengths in Careers **79**
- ❖ *Channeling Hyperfocus for Career Advancement* **80**
- ❖ *Creative Problem-Solving with ADHD* **83**
- ❖ *Turning Impulsivity into Quick Decision-Making* **87**
- ❖ *Resilience and Adaptability as Career Strengths* **91**

Chapter 6: Multitasking and Workload Management **102**
- ❖ *Prioritization Frameworks for the ADHD Mind* **103**

- ❖ *Setting Clear Boundaries Between Tasks* **106**
- ❖ *Focus Blocks: Single-Tasking in a Multitasking World* **109**
- ❖ *Delegation Skills for People with ADHD* **113**

Chapter 7: Kickstarting and Sustaining Projects **121**
- ❖ *Maintaining Momentum in Long-Term Projects* **125**
- ❖ *Setting and Achieving Short-Term Milestones* **128**
- ❖ *Reward Systems to Enhance Productivity* **132**

Chapter 8: Advanced Networking and Social Skills **139**
- ❖ *Mastering Small Talk with ADHD* **140**
- ❖ *Reading Social Cues in Professional Settings* **143**
- ❖ *Building and Maintaining Professional Relationships* **146**
- ❖ *Strategies for Effective Online Networking* **149**

Chapter 9: Personal Success Stories **158**
- ❖ *Success in the Arts: Harnessing Creativity* **159**
- ❖ *Achievements in the Sciences: Detail Orientation* **163**
- ❖ *Leadership in Business: Using ADHD to Innovate* **167**
- ❖ *Military Precision: ADHD in Structured Environments* ... **171**

Chapter 10: Tailored Strategies for Specific Careers **181**
- ❖ *ADHD in Creative Professions: Managing Unstructured Time* **182**
- ❖ *ADHD in Technology Fields: Coping with Constant Change* **186**
- ❖ *ADHD in Education: Strategies for Teachers* **190**
- ❖ *ADHD in Healthcare: Managing High-Stress Environments* **194**

Chapter 11: Integrating Technology and Tools **203**
- ❖ *Apps for Time Management and Focus* **204**
- ❖ *Tools for Organizational Efficiency* **207**
- ❖ *Gadgets That Improve Workplace Productivity* **211**
- ❖ *Using Social Media for Professional Growth* **215**

Chapter 12: Long-Term Career Planning with ADHD **224**
- ❖ *Setting Career Goals with ADHD* **225**

- ❖ *Long-Term Skill Development Strategies*...**228**
- ❖ *Preparing for Career Transitions*...**231**
- ❖ *Building a Personal Brand with ADHD*...**235**

Conclusion ...**243**
- ❖ *Keeping the Game Alive*...**249**

References ...**250**

Introduction

"Success is to be measured not so much by the position that one has reached in life as by the obstacles which he has overcome."

— **Booker T. Washington**

My life took a wild, unexpected twist on a crisp autumn morning in my mid-thirties back in 2019. Picture this: I'm sitting in a room that could pass for a paper factory, surrounded by towering stacks of psychological evaluations, when I hear the words, "Your wife and son have ADHD." It was like being hit by a thunderbolt from a far-off storm—shocking, yet suddenly everything made sense. This wasn't the end of the story; it was the thrilling prologue to a whole new chapter. I began to see my wife and son not as struggling against the tide but as untapped reservoirs of pure, unfiltered potential.

Growing up in the fast-paced, vibrant mosaic that is Brooklyn, NY I got used to navigating a world where distractions were as common as corner bodegas. For years, I watched my wife and son wrestle with their hyperactivity and distractibility, viewing them as hurdles that set them apart from their peers. But that fateful morning, I realized those traits weren't flaws—they were supercharged batteries of energy and creativity. I saw my wife dominate in finance and data analysis while others floundered like fish out of water. Simple chores that I breezed through were Herculean tasks for her, and vice versa, that's why I guess we match. And my son? The same genes as his mother, he's got superpowers that are waiting to be discovered, no cape required, and one day he'll channel them into whatever career he chooses.

This book is built on a game-changing thesis: ADHD can be your professional superpower if you know how to harness it. I'm laying out a roadmap to transform what many see as a setback into your greatest career asset. Packed with practical, evidence-based strategies tailored to your unique strengths, this guide is your ticket to career advancement.

We'll start by diving into the unique brain wiring of people with ADHD, explaining why conventional workplace methods often fall flat. From there, we'll cover custom time management systems, organizational hacks, and strategies to keep your focus sharp in meetings—all designed with your specific needs in mind. Later sections will delve into emotional regulation, stress management, and building a powerhouse professional network, ending with real-life success stories that prove embracing your ADHD can be transformational.

Get ready to flip the script on ADHD and turn it into your secret weapon for professional success. My goal for this book is to help you, career adults with ADHD, find and use your particular abilities. You'll find "ADHD-friendly strategies" that are more than simply advice; they demonstrate what can be accomplished when we adjust our mindset and deliberately employ our natural abilities.

Importantly, each chapter focuses on real-life applications and provides concrete recommendations. These aren't abstract theories; they're practical tools you can use right away to boost your professional and personal life.

As we work through these pages together, I hope to provide you with both understanding and practical assistance. Allow this book to be a beacon for you, as understanding their ADHD was for me, revealing a road to not only achieve but flourish in your career. Let us reinvent what it means to live and work with ADHD by embracing every difficulty as an opportunity to grow.

My Motivation

Over the years, I've navigated the complexities of ADHD, uncovering its weaknesses, strengths, and everything in between. This journey inspired me to write this book to share these insights with you and countless other adults living with ADHD. I understand that what many of you are seeking now is a solution, a way to cope, or strategies to achieve your fullest potential. If you ask me, the first step is YOU. Your willingness to understand your own mind and harness your unique abilities is what will truly make the difference.

I wrote this book to share some secrets you might not find elsewhere. The difference between individuals with and without ADHD often lies in the level of self-awareness, support, and the tools they use to navigate their environment. This book explores what to expect when managing an inattentive or impulsive disorder and how you can leverage your strengths. You'll discover potential causes, risk factors, and practical strategies to thrive despite the challenges.

Let's embark on this journey together and unlock your potential!

Chapter 1:

Mastering Time Management

"Don't think about what can happen in a month. Don't think about what can happen in a year. Just focus on the 24 hours in front of you and do what you can to get closer to where you want to be!"

– Eric Thomas

Have you ever felt like a circus juggler with one too many flaming torches in the air, desperately trying not to get burned? That's daily life for many people with ADHD, right? Time management might seem like a mythical beast we've all heard of but never actually seen. But here's the good news: it's not only real, it can actually be tamed and turned into one of your best allies.

Managing time effectively can feel like trying to pin down a cloud for professionals with ADHD. It's elusive, and just when you think you've got a handle on it, it morphs into a different shape. But what if I told you that the secret weapon lies in harnessing the power of visual tools? Yes, turning the abstract concept of time into something you can see and almost touch might just be the game-changer we've been looking for.

1.1 Visual Time Management Tools for the ADHD Mind

Introduction of Visual Tools

For individuals with ADHD, visual stimuli play a crucial role in enhancing cognitive processing. It's like giving a camera lens a good clean—suddenly everything comes into focus. Visual tools such as timers, color-coded calendars, and graphical task lists can transform the nebulous concept of time into a tangible element that you can organize, manipulate, and master.

These tools capitalize on our inherent strength in processing visual information—a common trait among many who have ADHD. By making tasks visually distinct and time perceptible, these tools help bridge the gap between intention and action, a common stumbling block for many of us.

Step-by-step Guide on Setting Up Visual Systems

Setting up a visual time management system can be a fun and creative process. Start with identifying the tools that resonate most with you. For some, the simplicity of a Kanban board might be appealing. This Japanese invention uses cards or notes moved across a board to track progress. For others, digital apps that integrate color-coding and graphical representations of tasks can provide the necessary structure.

Choose Your Tool: Whether it's a physical board or a digital app, pick a tool that you find intuitive and enjoyable to use.

Categorize Tasks: Break your responsibilities into categories. Each category should have a distinct color or symbol. This could be 'Work', 'Home', 'Personal Development', etc.

Prioritize Visually: Within each category, organize tasks by priority. Use positioning (top to bottom) or different shades of the same color to denote urgency.

Time Indicators: If using a digital tool, set up alerts or alarms that provide a visual cue when it's time to start a new task or take a break. For physical boards, you might place a timer nearby that can be reset for each new task.

Real-life Applications

Imagine starting your day with a clear visual map of what lies ahead. On your Kanban board, you have a bright yellow card at the top labeled "Morning Meeting", followed by a green card for "Project Research" and a red card for "Emails" slotted just before lunch. Each task is allocated a specific time frame, visible at a glance.

This method not only helps in structuring your day but also provides the satisfaction of moving completed tasks to a 'Done' section—nothing beats the visual affirmation of seeing your progress pile up.

Customization Tips for Various Work Environments

The beauty of visual time management tools lies in their flexibility. For those in a dynamic sales role, digital tools that sync across multiple devices can be a lifesaver, ensuring you're always on top of your schedule, whether you're at the office or out meeting clients. Creative professionals, on the other hand, might benefit from a more free-form Kanban board that allows the space to add, rearrange, and remove tasks as inspiration strikes.

In each case, the key is to adapt the system to fit your workflow. If you find yourself ignoring digital reminders, try incorporating a physical element like a desktop timer. Or if your workspace is too chaotic for a large board, consider a compact digital version that can provide the same visual cues without the clutter.

Through these strategies, visual time management tools not only cater to our need for external structure but also tap into the ADHD brain's affinity for visual thinking, making them an indispensable ally in our quest to conquer time and boost productivity.

1.2 Breaking Large Projects into Manageable Tasks

Ever stared at a project so big it felt like you were at the foot of Everest, wearing flip-flops? That's a familiar scene for those indiviuduals with ADHD. The sheer scale of large tasks can be paralyzing. But here's a little secret: the trick isn't to scale the mountain in one giant leap, but to create a series of smaller hills that are much easier to climb. Breaking down mammoth tasks into bite-sized pieces isn't just a good project management technique, it's a psychological lifeline for adults with ADHD.

Understanding Task Breakdown

When you break a large project into manageable tasks, it does something wonderful to your brain. It reduces the cognitive load - that feeling of mental overcrowding - and replaces it with clarity and focus. Each small, clear task feels achievable, and every time you tick one off your list, your brain gets a hit of dopamine - that feel-good hormone that says, 'Hey, nice job!' This not only boosts your mood but also fuels your motivation to keep going. It turns an overwhelming project into a series of victories, which is exactly what we need to keep our brains engaged and happy.

Techniques for Effective Breakdown

So, how do you eat an elephant? One bite at a time. Start with the 'divide and conquer' technique. For instance, if you're working on launching a new product, divide the project into phases like Research, Design, Production, and Marketing. Each of these phases can be broken down further into smaller tasks. Research might include market analysis, competitor evaluation, and customer surveys. The key is to make each task specific and actionable.

For those who thrive with tech, leveraging project management software can be a game changer. Tools like Asana or Trello allow you to create task hierarchies, making it easy to visualize the breakdown from phases to individual tasks. You can assign deadlines and priorities, and even share the tasks with team members, keeping everyone on the same page.

Incorporating Milestones and Checkpoints

Milestones are your road signs on the highway of project management. They guide you and give you points to aim for. Setting up milestones helps you gauge your progress and gives you opportunities to review and adjust your plan if necessary. For example, if your project is to write a book, a milestone could be completing the outline, then finishing each chapter. These checkpoints serve as motivational markers, celebrating your progress, which is incredibly important to maintain momentum in longer projects.

Visualization of Progress

There's something incredibly satisfying about seeing your progress visually. It's like watching your character level up in a video game. Tools like Gantt charts or progress bars in project management apps can give you this visual feedback. They map out your project timeline and show you how each piece of the puzzle fits together and progresses over time. Watching your progress bar inch closer to completion with each task you complete can be a real boost, especially on days when your motivation is waning.

By breaking down daunting projects into smaller, manageable tasks and visually tracking your progress, you not only make the work more approachable but also turn the process into a series of small wins. And let's face it, winning feels great, doesn't it? It keeps us going, especially when the road is long. Each small task completed is a step forward, a tangible proof that yes, you are moving, you are achieving, you are climbing your Everest—one small, well-equipped step at a time.

1.3 Overcoming Time Blindness with Simple Techniques

Have you ever planned to start a task at a certain time, only to look up and realize hours have slipped by unnoticed? Or perhaps you've underestimated how long a project would take and found yourself scrambling at the last minute? Welcome to the world of time blindness, a common challenge for professionals with ADHD. Time blindness is essentially a difficulty in perceiving and managing the passage of time. It can make us perennial latecomers or the people who are still working when everyone else has packed up and gone home. This isn't just about quirky mishaps; it impacts our professional credibility and personal well-being, often leading to stress and frustration.

But here's a slice of good news—time blindness isn't insurmountable. With some clever strategies, we can improve our relationship with time. One effective approach is to use alarms and countdown timers. Think of these as friendly nudges rather than the old school bell that used to jar us out of our daydreams. By setting alarms at regular intervals—say, every half hour or so—they can prompt us to check in with our current task, assess how much we've accomplished, and decide if we need to speed up, slow down, or switch gears. And here's a tip: vary the alarm tones. Our brains can get used to a sound if it's repeated too often and start ignoring it, so mixing it up can keep things fresh.

Now, let's talk about the power of daily planning rituals. This isn't about filling every minute of your day with tasks like some kind of productivity robot. Instead, it's about taking a moment each morning to outline your key goals for the day. Use tools that provide both auditory and visual feedback—there are plenty of apps that can help with this. Visual planners can show your day at a glance, while auditory cues can remind you of upcoming meetings or deadlines as they approach. This ritual helps create a mental map of your day, making the invisible passage of time a bit more visible and tangible. Plus, crossing off completed tasks provides a visual reward, reinforcing your sense of progress and control over time.

Implementing these techniques consistently can lead to significant improvements in your time awareness and management. Over time, you might find yourself feeling less rushed and more in control of your day. It's like developing a new sense, one that allows you to navigate your day with more assurance and less stress. Imagine being able to finish your work with enough time to spare for a coffee break or a walk. Or not feeling the panic monster breathing down your neck as a deadline approaches because you've paced your work effectively. These aren't just pleasant scenarios; they can become your reality with the right approaches to managing time blindness.

Remember, the goal here isn't to morph into a time-obsessed productivity machine. Instead, it's about finding ways to work with time rather than feeling like it's always working against you. These strategies are not about constraining your creativity or spontaneity but about giving them a framework in which they can thrive without causing chaos in your professional life or personal peace. So, give these techniques a try and see how they can transform your relationship with time from frenemy to ally, making your days both more productive and less pressured.

1.4 The Pomodoro Technique Adapted for ADHD

Imagine discovering a simple tool that transforms the relentless tick-tock of your workday into a series of small victories. That's the magic of the Pomodoro Technique, especially when it's tailored to fit the unique rhythm of an ADHD brain. Originating from the Italian word for 'tomato', this method was developed by Francesco Cirillo in the late 1980s and involves breaking work into intervals, traditionally 25 minutes in length, separated by short breaks. Each interval is known as a "Pomodoro", named after the tomato-shaped kitchen timer Cirillo used as a university student.

For professionals with ADHD, the traditional Pomodoro intervals might feel like a straitjacket rather than a tool for productivity. Our attention spans and work rhythms aren't always neatly packaged into standard quarter-hour blocks. Therefore, adapting the length of both focus periods and breaks to better suit our natural ebb and flow can make all the difference. Some might find that a 15-minute focus followed by a 5-minute break works better, or perhaps a 45-minute-deep dive into a task with a 15-minute break to recharge is more up your alley.

Incorporating technology can further enhance the Pomodoro Technique for ADHD needs. Apps like Focus Keeper or Tomato Timer allow customization of time intervals and can send reminders when it's time to start or stop a session. These digital tools help keep us on track without the cognitive overload of watching the clock. They free up mental space for the work at hand, providing just enough structure to guide us through the day without overwhelming our brains.

Let's look at how real individuals have turned this adapted Pomodoro Technique into a cornerstone of their professional productivity. Take Michael, a graphic designer, who discovered that traditional Pomodoro intervals were too short for his creative flow. By adjusting his focus periods to 40 minutes, he found a rhythm that allowed him to fully immerse himself in designing without hitting the mental "wall" that often comes with longer periods. His breaks, extended to 10 minutes, provided ample time to step away, refresh his mind, and return ready for another round of focused creativity.

Similarly, Sarah, a software developer, uses a modified Pomodoro Technique to tackle her coding work. She found that shorter intervals of 20 minutes of coding followed by 5 minutes of physical activity—like stretching or a quick walk—kept her more engaged and less prone to distraction. This frequent shifting between mental and physical engagement helped maintain her concentration throughout the day, reducing the fatigue that typically set in during the afternoon.

These examples underscore the versatility and effectiveness of the Pomodoro Technique when adapted for ADHD. By playing around with the duration of work and break intervals and using technology to keep the rhythm, individuals with ADHD can create a personalized approach to productivity that respects their unique needs and harnesses their dynamic energy. This methodology doesn't just help in ticking off tasks from a to-do list; it builds a workflow that can accommodate the intense highs and frustrating lows of ADHD, turning time management from a daily struggle into a series of manageable, and even enjoyable, moments.

So, as you consider the tools and strategies that best support your work style, remember that the goal is to find what genuinely works for you—something that respects the natural pace at which you perform best. Whether you're coding software, crafting marketing strategies, or even planning your next art project, the adapted Pomodoro Technique offers a flexible framework to explore productivity on your own terms. It invites you to experiment with time, to play with your schedule, and to discover the most satisfying and effective way to engage with your tasks. After all, productivity is personal, and when you find the right rhythm, your workday can transform into a dance that feels both spontaneous and structured, energetic and balanced.

Key Takeaways

1.1 Visual Time Management Tools

- Visual stimuli enhance cognitive processing for ADHD individuals.
- Tools like timers, color-coded calendars, and graphical task lists make time tangible.
- Setup involves choosing a tool, categorizing tasks, prioritizing visually, and using time indicators.
- Customization is key to fitting various work environments.

1.2 Breaking Large Projects into Manageable Tasks

- Reducing cognitive load by breaking tasks down improves focus and motivation.
- Techniques include dividing tasks into phases and using project management software.
- Milestones and checkpoints guide progress and provide motivational markers.
- Visual progress tracking through Gantt charts or progress bars boosts motivation.

1.3 Overcoming Time Blindness

- Time blindness leads to difficulty in perceiving and managing time.
- Strategies include using alarms and countdown timers, and establishing daily planning rituals.
- Daily planning creates a mental map of the day and reinforces a sense of progress.
- Consistent implementation leads to improved time awareness and reduced stress.

1.4 The Pomodoro Technique Adapted for ADHD

- The Pomodoro Technique involves breaking work into intervals with breaks.
- Adapting interval lengths to fit individual attention spans enhances effectiveness.
- Technology can customize and remind users of work and break periods.
- Examples show success in tailoring intervals to personal work rhythms, improving focus and reducing fatigue.

Chapter 2:

Organizational Systems That Work

"The first step in crafting the life you want is to get rid of everything you don't."

- Joshua Becker

Ever walked into a room and completely forgotten why you were there? Now, imagine that room is your workspace, and the forgotten 'why' is the crucial task you were supposed to finish. Sound familiar? Then you, my friend, might be wrestling with the chaos demon known as clutter. Clutter isn't just a physical mess; it's a productivity vampire that sucks the life out of your focus and energy, especially if you have ADHD. It turns your workspace into a battlefield of distractions. But fear not! We're about to embark on an epic decluttering crusade to reclaim your space and your sanity. Grab your metaphorical sword and shield, and let's conquer that clutter once and for all!

2.1 Decluttering Strategies for the Chronically Disorganized

Understanding the Impact of Clutter

Clutter is like that one guest at your party who eats all the snacks, spills drinks everywhere, and won't leave even after the music stops. In your workspace, clutter consumes your attention and energy, leaving less for the tasks that matter. For professionals with ADHD, whose minds are already whirlwinds of activity, additional chaos can lead to increased anxiety and diminished productivity. It's not just about being tidy; it's about creating an environment where our brains can function at their best. Visual chaos leads to mental chaos, and that's the last thing we need when trying to focus.

Step-by-Step Decluttering Process

Tackling a mountain of clutter might seem daunting, but fear not! The trick is not to try to clean up everything at once. Start small—choose one area or even one drawer to organize first. It's like training for a marathon; you wouldn't run 26 miles on your first day.

Choose Your Spot: Start with something manageable. Perhaps it's your desk surface or that infamous 'junk' drawer.

1. **Sort Ruthlessly**: Create three categories: Keep, Donate/Sell, and Trash. Be merciless. If you haven't used something in the past year, it's unlikely you'll need it tomorrow.
2. **Organize What Remains**: For the items you keep, find a logical place for each thing. Group like items together so you always know where to find them.

This method reduces the overwhelm by breaking the task into small, manageable chunks. And there's something incredibly satisfying about seeing a clear, organized space emerge from the chaos.

Tools and Techniques for Effective Decluttering

Now that you've started, let's make sure you have the right tools for the job. Label makers can be your new best friends. Seriously, these little gadgets are like magic wands that transform a sea of indistinct items into a neatly organized system. Label your shelves, bins, and folders, and watch as chaos turns into calm.

For digital clutter, think of decluttering software like CleanMyMac or CCleaner as your personal computer doctors, clearing out those files clogging your computer's arteries. Your digital workspace will breathe easier, and so will you.

When it comes to physical items, let frequency be your guide. If you use something daily, it should be within arm's reach, not buried in a drawer or hidden behind a stack of papers. Items you use less frequently can be stored away. This 'usage-based' organization mimics how our brains prioritize information, making it easier to find what you need without unnecessary searching. It's like giving your workspace a brain-friendly makeover!

Maintaining a Clutter-Free Environment

The key to maintaining order is regular check-ups. Schedule a monthly decluttering session to revisit and reorganize. Embrace the minimalist mantra of "one in, one out." Every time a new item comes into your space, make it a rule to let go of another. Not only does this keep your clutter in check, but it also makes you think twice about what you bring into your space.

Consider this approach a form of self-care. A clutter-free environment leads to a clearer mind, reducing stress and enhancing your ability to focus. Plus, there's an undeniable thrill in opening a drawer and finding exactly what you need, exactly when you need it—no treasure map needed.

By integrating these decluttering strategies into your routine, you create more than just a tidy workspace. You construct a haven of productivity that supports your ADHD brain, making it easier to focus and excel in your professional endeavors. Whether you're crafting a business plan, writing a report, or planning your next art project, a decluttered space sets the stage for unfettered creativity and efficiency. So, roll up your sleeves and reclaim your space—one paper pile and digital file at a time.

2.2 Digital Organization for the ADHD Professional

Let's face it: the digital world can be a labyrinth of distractions and disarray. Have you ever found yourself drowning in a sea of digital files, or maybe you've spent hours searching for that one crucial email buried under a mountain of spam? It's like every file and email is a gremlin that multiplies every time you look away. This digital chaos can be more than just a nuisance; it can genuinely hinder the ability to work effectively, leading to stress and a plummet in productivity. But don't worry, there's a method to the madness, and with a few strategic moves, we can turn that digital jungle into a well-manicured garden.

First up, let's tackle setting up a digital filing system. Think of this as mapping out your digital domain. The key here is to mimic the natural way your brain categorizes information. Start by creating broad categories that make sense for your work and personal life. These could be labels like 'Projects', 'Finances', 'Personal', and 'Miscellaneous'. Under each of these, you can create subfolders for more specific items. For example, under 'Projects', you might have subfolders for each client or project you're currently working on.

When setting up these folders, keep the structure intuitive. The goal is to reduce the time you spend hunting for files, so organize them in a way that feels natural to you. This might mean arranging folders by priority, project phase, or even the type of task. Whatever system you choose, the aim is to make it so that even on your busiest days, when your ADHD is doing its best to keep you off track, you can find what you need without a fuss.

Now, let's talk about email, which for many of us is a constant source of anxiety and distraction. Managing your email effectively is like keeping a dragon in a cage—it needs strong bars, or it's going to wreak havoc. Setting up email filters is a great start. Most email services allow you to create rules that automatically sort incoming mail into relevant folders. You can have filters for different clients, projects, or even types of communication like invoices or meeting requests. This not only keeps your inbox tidy but also helps you prioritize which emails need your immediate attention.

Another handy technique is the use of flags or stars for emails that require actions or follow-ups. This visual cue can help you keep track of important messages and ensures nothing slips through the cracks. Regular inbox reviews are crucial—setting aside a specific time each day or week to go through your emails and organize them can prevent build-up and keep your digital communications streamlined.

Lastly, let's explore the digital tools that can further enhance our organizational efforts. Cloud storage services like Dropbox or Google Drive can be lifesavers. They not only keep your files backed up and secure but also allow you to access them from anywhere, which is perfect for those of us who are always on the go. Note-taking apps like Evernote or

OneNote are also fantastic for keeping all your thoughts, ideas, and to-dos in one place. And let's not forget about task management software like Asana or Trello, which can help you keep track of your projects and deadlines with visual boards and timelines.

These tools not only help in keeping your digital life organized but also sync across multiple devices, ensuring you have access to your information whether you're on your computer, tablet, or smartphone. This connectivity is crucial for maintaining flow and productivity, especially on days when ADHD might be pulling your attention in a thousand different directions.

By embracing these strategies and tools, the digital realm becomes less of a battlefield and more of a command center, where you can control the flow of information and manage your tasks with precision. The chaos of misplaced files and overwhelming inboxes can be tamed, leaving you more time and energy to focus on what truly matters—your work, your passions, and your wellbeing. So, dive into these digital organizing techniques and transform the way you interact with your tech environment. It's not just about being neat; it's about creating a space that supports your mind and your ambitions, helping you to thrive in all areas of your life.

2.3 Creating an ADHD-Friendly Workspace

Imagine stepping into a workspace that doesn't just 'get' you but actually helps channel your vibrant energy and creativity into productivity. That's the dream, right? Well, it's absolutely achievable. Creating an ADHD-friendly workspace goes beyond just having a tidy desk. It's about designing an environment that reduces distractions and enhances focus, particularly for those of us whose brains are perpetually buzzing with ideas.

Let's start with the basics: a minimalistic design. Now, minimalism doesn't mean your office has to look like a stark, white cube (unless that's your vibe). It's about simplicity and functionality. Each item in your workspace should have a purpose and a place. Why? Because every unnecessary item is potential fodder for distraction. Think about it! —how often have you found yourself fiddling with something on your desk instead of focusing on your work? By keeping the decor simple and the clutter to a minimum, you create a serene space where your brain can relax and focus on the tasks at hand.

Then there's the strategic placement of essential items. Keep frequently used items within easy reach to minimize the need to get up and hunt for things. This not only saves time but also helps maintain your focus. On the other hand, items that are rarely used shouldn't take up prime real estate on your desk. Store them away to keep your workspace clean and ready for action.

Reducing visual and auditory distractions is crucial. If you're easily distracted by movement, position your desk so that you face away from high-traffic areas. For noise distractions, noise-canceling headphones can be a game-changer, or perhaps a white noise machine to drown out disruptive sounds. The aim is to control the sensory input around you, allowing your mind to calm and focus on your work.

Now, let's talk about ergonomics and comfort, which are often overlooked but vital aspects of a productive workspace. Investing in an ergonomic chair that supports your back, a desk at the right height, and perhaps a footrest can significantly enhance your comfort and prevent strains or fatigue. Remember, physical discomfort is a distraction you don't need. Optimal lighting is also paramount—poor lighting can cause eye strain and headaches, sapping your energy and concentration. Natural light is ideal, but if that's not possible, ensure your artificial lighting is bright enough to work comfortably without being harsh.

The psychology of color can also play a significant role in your productivity. Different colors can evoke different moods and levels of alertness. For instance, blue is often seen as calming and can enhance productivity, while green might help you feel relaxed and refreshed. Consider the mood you want to foster in your workspace and choose your colors accordingly. This doesn't mean you need to repaint the whole room—small pops of color, whether from a piece of art, a rug, or desk accessories, can also do the trick.

Personalizing your workspace is about striking a balance. It's tempting to fill your desk with fun knick-knacks or inspirational quotes, but remember, every addition should serve a purpose. Maybe choose a select few personal items that motivate you or make you smile—like photos of loved ones, a plant to add some life and clean the air, or a special memento that reminds you of your goals. These personal touches should inspire you, not pull your focus away from work.

For instance, I keep a small, potted plant on my desk—its greenery not only brightens up my space but also reminds me to take mental breathers now and then. Plus, caring for it adds a simple, routine break in my workday that helps me regroup and refocus. Also, consider tools that aid in personal organization—maybe a bulletin board for important reminders or a digital tool that helps keep your deadlines in check.

Creating an ADHD-friendly workspace isn't about following a strict set of rules. It's about understanding what elements make you most productive and comfortable and implementing them in your environment. This personalized approach not only makes your workspace truly yours but also turns it into a powerhouse of productivity, tailored just for you. So, take the time to assess your needs and make those adjustments. Your brain—and your work—will thank you for it.

2.4 Routine Checklists to Maintain Order

Imagine you have a virtual assistant in your pocket, one that gently nudges you through your day with reminders and ticks off your achievements as you go. That's essentially what a checklist does for professionals with ADHD. It's more than just a list; it's a roadmap to daily success, a visual affirmation that yes, you are getting things done. Checklists externalize our memory, providing clear cues for what needs to be done and when, which is incredibly valuable when your brain tries to juggle several tasks at once.

Checklists serve a dual purpose. Not only do they help in managing day-to-day tasks, but they also play a crucial role in task initiation – often a significant hurdle for individuals with ADHD. The simple act of checking off a task provides a small yet meaningful reward, releasing a hit of dopamine – our brain's favorite feel-good neurotransmitter. This reward mechanism can help overcome the inertia that often accompanies the start of a new task. It's like having a cheerleader who celebrates each small victory with you, keeping you motivated throughout the day.

Designing these checklists, however, is where the real magic happens. A well-crafted checklist is clear, actionable, and visually appealing. Start by breaking down your tasks into specific actions. For instance, instead of writing 'Report on project,' break it down to 'Gather data for project report,' 'Draft report outline,' and 'Write report introduction.' This method makes each step manageable and precise. For the visual appeal, use colors or icons to categorize tasks— perhaps red for urgent tasks, blue for emails, and green for personal errands. This not only makes your checklist pleasing to look at but also allows you to scan and prioritize tasks quickly.

Integrating these checklists into your daily routine can be transformative. Place your checklist somewhere you can't miss it—like on your fridge door or as the wallpaper on your phone or computer. Make it the first thing you see in the morning and the last thing you check before you end your day. Regularly update your checklist, adding new tasks as they come and ticking off completed ones. This habit not only keeps your list functional but also turns it into a living document of your daily productivity.

Now, when it comes to choosing between digital and paper checklists, consider your personal style and needs. Paper checklists are tangible. There's something inherently satisfying about physically crossing off a task that can make you feel more connected to your accomplishments. They're also free from digital distractions—no notifications popping up just as you're reviewing what needs to be done. However, they are not as easily editable and can be cumbersome to carry around if your list is lengthy.

Digital checklists, on the other hand, offer flexibility and convenience. Apps like Todoist or Microsoft To Do can send reminders, sync across all your devices, and are easily adjustable. They're perfect for on-the-go lifestyles and can be integrated with other digital tools you use. However, they do carry the risk of leading you into a digital distraction rabbit hole. The choice between digital and paper ultimately depends on your personal preference and the nature of your tasks. Some find a hybrid approach works best—using digital checklists for work and paper for personal tasks.

By making checklists a cornerstone of your daily routine, you transform them from mere tools to trusted allies in your quest for productivity and order. They become the framework around which you can structure your day, providing clarity and a sense of control that can sometimes feel elusive when your brain is spinning with the responsibilities of life.

As we wrap up this chapter, remember that the strategies discussed here are more than just organizational tactics; they are stepping stones to a more structured, productive, and mentally satisfying lifestyle. Checklists are your partners in this journey, guiding you through your daily tasks and ensuring that nothing slips through the cracks. As you move forward, these tools will not only help you manage your tasks but also boost your confidence in your ability to handle the complexities of life with ADHD.

Looking ahead, we will dive deeper into strategies for managing stress and emotions, crucial skills for maintaining not just productivity but also your overall well-being. Let's continue to build on the foundation we've set here, exploring ways to thrive not just in work but in all areas of life.

Key Takeaways

2.1 Decluttering Strategies for the Chronically Disorganized

- **Impact of Clutter:** Clutter consumes attention and energy, leading to increased anxiety and diminished productivity for professionals with ADHD.
- **Step-by-Step Decluttering:** Start small, sort items into Keep, Donate/Sell, and Trash categories, and organize what remains.
- **Tools and Techniques:** Use label makers and decluttering software, organize by usage frequency, and mimic brain prioritization.
- **Maintaining Order:** Schedule monthly decluttering sessions, embrace "one in, one out" rule, and view decluttering as self-care.

2.2 Digital Organization for the ADHD Professional

- **Digital Filing System:** Create intuitive categories and subfolders to reduce time spent hunting for files.
- **Email Management:** Set up filters, use flags or stars, and conduct regular inbox reviews to keep emails organized.

- **Digital Tools:** Utilize cloud storage, note-taking apps, and task management software for better organization and accessibility.
- **Overall Goal:** Turn digital chaos into a command center, improving productivity and reducing stress.

2.3 Creating an ADHD-Friendly Workspace

- **Minimalistic Design:** Keep decor simple and functional to minimize distractions.
- **Essential Items:** Keep frequently used items within easy reach and store rarely used items away.
- **Reduce Distractions:** Position desk away from high-traffic areas and use noise-canceling headphones or white noise machines.
- **Ergonomics and Comfort:** Invest in ergonomic furniture and optimal lighting to prevent discomfort and fatigue.
- **Color Psychology:** Use colors that enhance productivity and mood.
- **Personalization:** Balance personal items that motivate without causing distractions.

2.4 Routine Checklists to Maintain Order

- **Checklist Benefits:** Checklists serve as external memory, providing clear cues and rewarding task completion with dopamine.
- **Designing Checklists:** Break tasks into specific actions, use colors or icons for categorization, and update regularly.
- **Integration:** Place checklists in visible areas and update them frequently.
- **Digital vs. Paper:** Choose based on personal preference; digital offers flexibility and reminders, paper avoids digital distractions.

Chapter 3:

Navigating Professional Settings

"The most powerful person in the room is the one who remains calm and collected."

- Anonymous

Ah, professional settings—those arenas where the corporate gladiators battle, and the creative maestros perform. For professionals with ADHD, these environments can feel like a maze rigged with distraction traps and focus-stealers. But what if I told you that with the right strategies, you can not only survive but thrive in these settings? Yes, it's absolutely possible, and this chapter is your map to mastering the art of staying engaged, especially when meetings seem like marathons and your attention feels like it's on a 5-second leash.

3.1 Strategies for Staying Engaged in Meetings

Active Participation Techniques

Let's kick things off with active participation, a golden ticket to keeping your brain on track during meetings. You know how easy it is to drift off when someone else is speaking, especially if they're on slide 27 of a PowerPoint presentation. Active participation is the anchor that keeps your attention moored. It involves more than just being physically present in the room; it's about engaging actively—asking questions, taking notes, or even volunteering to lead a part of the discussion.

Why does this work? Well, when you engage actively, you signal to your brain that 'Hey, this is important!' This helps in ramping up your focus. Taking notes is particularly handy. It's like translating a foreign movie in real-time; it forces you to process information as it comes, keeping you tuned in. And if you're brave enough to ask questions or lead a part, you're essentially turning the spotlight onto yourself, a surefire way to keep your brain from wandering off.

Preparation Tips Before Meetings

Now, onto preparation, which can be a game-changer. Ever walked into a meeting room without a clue about the agenda and felt like you were trying to catch a train already speeding away? Yep, we've all been there. To avoid this, make it a habit to review the meeting agenda beforehand. Know what's going to be discussed and jot down any questions or comments you might want to add. This prep work doesn't just keep you informed; it makes you a contributor, someone who adds value to the discussion.

Setting personal goals for each meeting can also be incredibly effective. Maybe you decide that your goal is to provide feedback on a project or to learn something new related to your role. Having these goals in mind provides a lens through which to view the meeting, filtering the information and interactions in a way that aligns with your objectives.

Using Technology Aids

In our digital age, technology can be a double-edged sword, but when used wisely, it's an invaluable ally. Consider using meeting management apps like Microsoft Teams or Asana, which help you track discussion points and action items.

These tools are like having an extra brain to store everything important—freeing up your actual brain to engage in the moment.

For those of us who might struggle with auditory processing or who find visual aids helpful, these apps often allow for real-time note-taking and task assignments, which can be a lifesaver. They keep you plugged into the flow of the meeting, even when your ADHD tries to pull you away.

Physical Techniques to Maintain Alertness

Last but not least, let's talk about physical techniques to keep your body as engaged as your mind. Ever tried strategic seating? Choosing where you sit in a meeting can significantly impact your engagement level. Sitting at the front can reduce distractions and make it easier to maintain focus on the speaker. If you're prone to feeling restless, sitting near the door can be helpful, giving you the freedom to step out for a quick stretch without causing a commotion.

And then there are the fidget tools—stress balls, fidget spinners, or even doodling can help maintain your physical focus without distracting others. For the more adventurous, why not try a standing desk? Standing during a meeting can keep your body active and your mind alert, making it easier to stay engaged.

By incorporating these strategies into your meeting routines, you transform them from snooze-fests into dynamic sessions where your ADHD traits are not a liability but a leveraged asset. Meetings become not just something you have to endure but a platform where you can shine, using your unique abilities to actively contribute and soak in knowledge. So gear up with these techniques, and turn every meeting into an opportunity to display the full spectrum of your professional prowess.

3.2 Managing Workplace Relationships with ADHD

Navigating workplace relationships can sometimes feel like you're trying to dance a tango on a boat in choppy waters—especially when ADHD is in the mix. You might find that your natural spontaneity and zesty energy, while often infectious, can occasionally trip you up in the professional world. Understanding how ADHD symptoms such as impulsivity, forgetfulness, and emotional dysregulation can affect your interactions is the first step towards managing these relationships more effectively.

Impulsivity might mean you blurt out ideas in meetings without fully forming them first, or perhaps forgetfulness shows up as missing deadlines or being unprepared for presentations. Then there's emotional dysregulation, which might see you reacting more intensely to feedback than your colleagues expect. Each of these can strain relationships, leading to misunderstandings or friction. It's not just about you managing your ADHD; it's also about helping those around you understand where you're coming from, which can foster a more supportive working environment.

Building trust and understanding with colleagues doesn't happen overnight, especially when ADHD traits sometimes paint a skewed picture of your capabilities or intentions. Being open about your ADHD, where appropriate, can be beneficial. It's not about making excuses but rather about clarifying your challenges so others can understand your perspective. For instance, explaining that your occasional forgetfulness is not a sign of disinterest but a part of your ADHD might encourage colleagues to remind you of deadlines gently, rather than getting frustrated. This transparency can build empathy and even encourage your teammates to come to you with their own struggles, creating a deeper mutual understanding.

Conflict is almost inevitable in any workplace, but when you add ADHD into the mix, the waters can get particularly choppy. Effective conflict resolution techniques are crucial. Active listening is at the heart of this—really hearing what the other person is saying without immediately jumping to your own defense. It's about taking a breath before responding, allowing yourself a moment to process the information and manage your emotions. This can help in crafting a more considered response and shows the other party that you value their perspective, which can defuse tension and lead to more productive resolutions.

Maintaining professional boundaries is also key. ADHD can sometimes blur these lines—spontaneity and a penchant for open, friendly relationships can inadvertently lead to over-sharing or stepping into personal territories too quickly. Setting clear boundaries for yourself and respecting others' limits can help in maintaining a professional demeanor. This might mean deciding beforehand what personal information is office-appropriate or recognizing when a friendly banter is veering into uncomfortable territory. Communicating these boundaries clearly and respectfully ensures everyone is on the same page, which helps in building a safe and comfortable environment for everyone.

In managing these aspects of workplace relationships, you not only make your day-to-day interactions smoother but also position yourself as a reliable and considerate colleague. It turns potential ADHD pitfalls into opportunities for fostering stronger, more understanding professional relationships, which are fundamental to both personal job satisfaction and career advancement.

3.3 Techniques for Effective Professional Communication

When it comes to professional communication, think of yourself as a chef. Just as a chef adjusts their techniques based on the ingredients and the desired dish, effective communication requires you to tailor your methods according to the information you need to convey and the audience you're addressing. Let's start with the foundation—structuring your communication. Whether you're firing off a quick email or preparing for a major presentation, organizing your thoughts can be your anchor amidst the whirlwind of ideas that ADHD often brings.

Imagine this: before you speak in a meeting or write an email, take a moment to jot down your main points. This can be as simple as a few bullet points on a sticky note or a more detailed outline on your laptop. The act of organizing your thoughts in this way does two things. First, it clarifies your message, not just for your recipients but for you as well. It's like putting on glasses that bring the world into focus. Suddenly, you see clearly what you need to communicate and why. Second, this preparation helps to keep your ADHD traits of impulsivity and tangential thinking in check, ensuring that your communication is coherent and on target.

Now, adapting your communication style to different audiences is crucial. Each audience has its own unique set of expectations and understanding. For instance, the way you explain a technical process to a room full of engineers can vastly differ from how you present it to a group of marketing professionals. The engineers might appreciate jargon and complex details, while the marketing team might benefit more from understanding the broader implications of the process on customer experience or sales outcomes. Switching between these styles isn't about being inauthentic; it's about respecting your audience's background and tailoring your message so it resonates and is understood.

Feedback, ah, the double-edged sword of professional growth—especially for professionals with ADHD, where a simple critique can feel like a personal attack, triggering defensive mechanisms. But here's a reframe: feedback is not a spotlight on your mistakes but a roadmap for improvement. When receiving feedback, first, breathe. Simple, right? But it's easy to forget when your brain is doing somersaults. Allow yourself the space to listen actively, without interrupting. Then, ask clarifying questions. This not only shows you are engaged but also helps you understand the feedback fully before responding. If you feel your emotions bubbling up, it's okay to ask for time to process the information. Responding with a cool head will always serve you better than a knee-jerk reaction.

Digital tools have revolutionized the way we communicate, but they can also be a pitfall for professionals with ADHD, tempting us with endless distractions. Yet, when used wisely, tools like email, instant messaging, and project management apps can enhance clarity and efficiency in communication. The key is to keep your digital communication clear and organized. Use subject lines effectively in emails, make your point right at the beginning, and use bullet points for important details. For instant messaging, keep your messages brief and to the point. Avoid the trap of informal banter that can lead to misunderstandings. With project management apps, make the most of features like task comments or update logs to keep everyone in the loop about project developments, reducing the need for lengthy meetings or email threads.

In wrapping up, think of these communication strategies as tools in your professional toolkit, each serving a specific purpose to help you build, maintain, and grow your workplace relationships and effectiveness. By structuring your communication, adapting to your audience, managing feedback constructively, and leveraging digital tools efficiently, you not only make your professional interactions more productive but also more enjoyable. After all, clear communication reduces misunderstandings and builds confidence—both in yourself and in the eyes of your colleagues. So, take these tools, tailor them to your needs, and watch as your professional communication transforms from a source of stress to a streamlined, effective component of your career success.

3.4 Handling Workplace Distractions

Let's talk distractions—a subject as familiar to us as our own reflections, especially in the workspace where they pop up more frequently than ads on a free streaming service. The workplace can sometimes feel like a minefield of potential distractions, each more enticing than the last. It might be the tantalizing buzz of conversation near the water cooler or the incessant pinging of app notifications that pull your focus away like a magnet. Identifying these distractions and their triggers is the first step in crafting your master plan to keep them at bay.

Start by pinpointing what grabs your attention most often, besides Instagram. Is it auditory distractions like the chatter from colleagues or the whirl of the coffee machine? Or perhaps visual distractions like the constant foot traffic past your desk? Recognizing these triggers helps in understanding your distraction patterns and preparing to counteract them. Once identified, you can start to build your arsenal of distraction-fighting tools. Noise-canceling headphones can be a game-changer for auditory interruptions, transforming your aural environment into a serene soundscape. For visual distractions, consider repositioning your workspace to face away from high-traffic areas or using a room divider to shield your line of sight from constant movement.

But let's dive deeper. Creating a "distraction-free zone" can be incredibly effective. This could mean setting up a specific area where only work-related activities occur. The physical separation of spaces assigns a psychological boundary, reinforcing to your brain that 'this space is for work'. During times when focus is paramount, consider utilizing tools like website blockers or setting your phone to 'Do Not Disturb' mode. These tools help create a virtual barrier, guarding your focus from the digital pings that so often pull us away from our tasks.

Structured breaks and time management also play crucial roles in maintaining focus. It might sound counterintuitive to take breaks to increase focus, but scheduled downtime can prevent burnout and keep your brain fresh. Consider the Pomodoro Technique, where you work for a set period—say, 25 minutes—and then break for five. These short breaks allow your mind to rest before taking on the next focused interval. Regular breaks not only cut down on the fatigue that comes from long stretches of focus but also provide designated times to indulge in less productive activities like checking social media or grabbing a coffee. This way, you satisfy your brain's craving for a distraction in a controlled, limited manner, which can prevent unscheduled time-wasting during focus periods.

Now, let's put all this into a personalized plan. Creating a "Distraction Management Plan" involves both preemptive strategies and reactive adjustments. Begin by setting clear goals for what you need to accomplish and the times you are most likely to be productive. Are mornings more productive for you, or are you an afternoon person? Use this information to schedule your most demanding tasks during your peak times. Next, incorporate the tools and techniques that work best for your specific distraction triggers, such as noise-canceling headphones or structured breaks.

But what happens when an unexpected distraction still breaks through your well-laid plans? Having a reactive strategy is key. This could be as simple as taking a deep breath and reminding yourself of the task at hand, or maybe it involves a quick reassessment of your environment—could moving to a quieter spot help? Perhaps re-engaging with your task post a quick walking break could reset your focus. The idea is to have a flexible toolkit of responses that you can tailor to different distraction scenarios.

By adopting these strategies, you not only minimize the impact of distractions but also enhance your ability to steer back to productivity swiftly and effectively. Handling distractions isn't about building an impenetrable fortress around your attention but rather about knowing how to guide it back when it strays, maintaining a balance between focus and freedom that supports your work and your ADHD.

As we wrap up this chapter, remember that managing distractions is about understanding your personal triggers, equipping yourself with the right tools, and being prepared to adapt as necessary. It's these strategies that will help you transform your workday from a series of frustration-filled moments to one of managed productivity and satisfaction. Now, as we move forward, let's continue to explore more ways to harness your unique skills and turn your work experience into not just a series of tasks, but a fulfilling part of your journey.

Key Takeaways

3.1 Strategies for Staying Engaged in Meetings

- **Active Participation:** Engage by asking questions, taking notes, and volunteering to lead discussions to maintain focus.
- **Preparation Tips:** Review the meeting agenda beforehand and set personal goals to stay informed and contribute effectively.
- **Technology Aids:** Use meeting management apps like Microsoft Teams or Asana for real-time note-taking and task tracking.
- **Physical Techniques:** Choose strategic seating, use fidget tools, or consider a standing desk to maintain alertness.

3.2 Managing Workplace Relationships with ADHD

- **Understanding Impact:** Recognize how ADHD symptoms like impulsivity, forgetfulness, and emotional dysregulation affect interactions.
- **Building Trust:** Be open about ADHD where appropriate to foster understanding and empathy among colleagues.

- **Conflict Resolution:** Practice active listening, take time to process feedback, and maintain professional boundaries.
- **Professional Boundaries:** Set clear boundaries for sharing personal information and respecting others' limits to maintain a professional demeanor.

3.3 Techniques for Effective Professional Communication

- **Structuring Communication:** Organize thoughts with bullet points or outlines to ensure clarity and coherence.
- **Adapting to Audiences:** Tailor communication style based on the audience's background and expectations.
- **Managing Feedback:** View feedback as a roadmap for improvement, ask clarifying questions, and respond after processing information.
- **Leveraging Digital Tools:** Use email subject lines effectively, keep messages concise, and utilize project management app features for clarity and efficiency.

3.4 Handling Workplace Distractions

- **Identifying Triggers:** Recognize common distractions and their triggers, such as auditory or visual interruptions.
- **Creating Distraction-Free Zones:** Set up specific areas for work-related activities and use tools like website blockers.
- **Structured Breaks:** Implement the Pomodoro Technique to balance focused work intervals with short breaks to prevent burnout.
- **Distraction Management Plan:** Schedule tasks during peak productivity times, use tools like noise-canceling headphones, and have reactive strategies for unexpected distractions.

Chapter 4:

Stress and Emotional Regulation

"Do not anticipate trouble, or worry about what may never happen. Keep in the sunlight."

- Benjamin Franklin

Imagine you're trying to juggle six oranges. Just as you think you've got the hang of it; someone tosses in a watermelon. That's a bit what managing stress with ADHD feels like—you're handling everyday stressors, and suddenly, a giant emotional melon comes your way, throwing everything off balance. But what if I told you that there's a way to not just juggle, but to do so with grace and maybe even a bit of flair? That's where mindfulness comes into play. It's not about clearing your mind or achieving Zen-like calm (although those are nice side benefits); it's about managing life's watermelons without letting them splat on the ground.

4.1 Mindfulness Practices for Stress Reduction

Introduction to Mindfulness

So, what exactly is mindfulness? At its core, mindfulness is about being present in the moment, fully engaging with what's happening, what you're doing, and the space you're moving through. For professionals with ADHD, whose minds are often racing through a hundred thoughts at once, this might sound like a tall order. But the beauty of mindfulness is that it's not about stopping these thoughts; it's about observing them without judgment and letting them pass without getting swept away in their current.

Why is this particularly beneficial for ADHD brains? Well, rapid thought processes and distractibility are our frequent companions, often leading to stress and emotional overwhelm. Mindfulness helps by training your brain to pause, observe, and choose how to respond rather than reacting impulsively. It's like installing a sophisticated software update in your mental operating system that improves your brain's ability to manage stress and regulate emotions.

Simple Mindfulness Exercises

Let's get practical with some mindfulness exercises you can easily weave into your workday. First up, breathing techniques—simple yet powerful. Try the "4-7-8" method: breathe in through your nose for 4 seconds, hold the breath for 7 seconds, and exhale slowly through your mouth for 8 seconds. This technique acts like a brake pedal for your nervous system, slowing everything down and bringing your focus back to the here and now.

Next, there's mindful listening, which can be a game-changer during meetings or conversations. This involves fully concentrating on the speaker, noticing the tone and pitch of their voice, the pauses between their words, and resisting the urge to plan your response while they're still talking. It's about listening to understand, not just to reply, which can significantly enhance your interpersonal interactions.

And don't forget about mindful walking—perfect for those short breaks between tasks. Imagine this: you're walking slowly and deliberately, feeling the sensation of each step, the weight transferring from heel to toe. It's like you're sneaking around your own office, but in a Zen kind of way.

It's a mini-vacation for your brain and a nice stretch for your legs. Plus, it's a great way to clear your mind and hit the reset button. So, the next time you need a break, take a mindful stroll. Who knows, you might just become the office guru of tranquility, ready to conquer tasks with newfound energy and a secret smile!

Integrating Mindfulness into Daily Routines

Incorporating mindfulness into your daily routine can start with something as simple as a morning session. Dedicate just five minutes each morning to sit quietly, close your eyes, and observe your breathing. This sets a calm, grounded tone for the day ahead. You can also use mindfulness cues before important tasks or meetings. Take a moment to ground yourself with a few deep breaths, or set an intention for how you want to approach the task. These small practices can make a significant difference in your stress levels and overall mental clarity.

Evaluating the Impact of Mindfulness

Now, you might be wondering, "Is all this mindfulness business really making a difference?" Here's where a bit of self-reflection comes into play. Keep a simple mindfulness journal. Each day, jot down a few notes about what mindfulness practices you tried, how they made you feel, and any changes you notice in your stress levels or focus. Over time, you'll be able to see patterns and perhaps identify particular techniques that are more effective for you. This ongoing evaluation not only keeps you engaged in your mindfulness journey but also steers you towards the practices that offer the most personal benefit.

Mindfulness Resource List

To further support your mindfulness practice, consider exploring the following resources:

- **Headspace**: An app offering guided meditations, including sessions specifically for focus and stress relief.
- **Insight Timer**: A free app with an extensive library of mindfulness exercises and guided meditations.
- **"Wherever You Go, There You Are" by Jon Kabat-Zinn**: A book that offers insightful, accessible perspectives on practicing mindfulness in everyday life.

By embracing mindfulness, you're not just learning to juggle the oranges and watermelons of life more adeptly; you're also opening up a space where stress is manageable and your reactions are thoughtful and deliberate. Mindfulness offers a way to navigate the chaos of daily life with a bit more ease and a lot less splat.

4.2 Cognitive Behavioral Techniques for Emotional Control

Let's shift gears to Cognitive Behavioral Therapy, or CBT as it's often called, a tool that might just become your new best friend in the workplace. At its heart, CBT is all about understanding the connections between thoughts, emotions, and behaviors, and then using this knowledge to bring about positive changes. Think of it like debugging a computer; CBT helps you identify and fix the 'bugs' in your thinking patterns that can cause emotional distress.

The core idea here is that our thoughts directly influence how we feel and behave. For professionals with ADHD, the brain can sometimes serve up a cocktail of overly negative thoughts that make stressful situations feel even worse. CBT teaches us to recognize these patterns, challenge them, and ultimately replace them with more accurate, constructive thoughts. It's about moving from a mindset of "I always mess up" to "Everyone makes mistakes, I can learn from this," which can drastically change how you feel and react in a situation.

Now, how do we apply CBT in the workplace? One powerful technique is cognitive restructuring, which involves identifying and challenging irrational beliefs. For instance, if you're terrified of giving presentations because you believe you'll humiliate yourself, cognitive restructuring helps you challenge that belief. Is it really true that you always mess up, or have there been times when you've done well? By examining the evidence for and against your belief, you can start to see that your fear might be based on distorted thinking.

Another handy tool is keeping a thought record. This is basically a diary where you jot down stressful situations, your thoughts about them, and the emotions you feel. Over time, you'll start to see patterns in your thinking that trigger negative emotions. Armed with this insight, you can begin to change how you think about and react to similar situations in the future. It's like being a detective in your own psychological thriller, where you're both the detective and the mystery to be solved.

But let's make this even more practical with some role-playing exercises. Imagine you're in a typical stressful work scenario—maybe you're dealing with a tight deadline. You can practice responding to this pressure in a low-risk setting, trying out different ways to manage your thoughts and emotions. Role-playing can be done with a therapist, a coach, or even a supportive colleague. The aim is to rehearse healthy responses so that when real-life work pressures mount, you're ready with strategies that keep your cool.

Building a CBT Toolkit

To really make CBT work for you, consider assembling a personal CBT toolkit. This can include key phrases that remind you to challenge your negative thoughts, like "Is this thought based on facts or feelings?" Keep these phrases on hand—maybe on a sticky note on your computer or in a note on your phone.

You might also include reminder cards that outline the steps for cognitive restructuring or instructions for keeping a thought record. These can serve as quick reference guides in moments of stress, helping you stay on track. Think of it as having a cheat sheet for your mental processes, one that helps you navigate through emotional turbulence with more agility and confidence.

Incorporating CBT into your daily work life can transform how you handle stress and interact with your colleagues. It equips you with a set of mental tools that not only improve your emotional well-being but also enhance your professional performance. By regularly practicing these techniques, you gradually shift your thinking patterns towards more positive and productive attitudes, which can make all the difference in a high-stakes business environment. So, explore CBT, practice its techniques, and watch as you start to handle workplace challenges with a newfound ease and effectiveness, turning stressful hurdles into opportunities for personal growth and professional excellence.

4.3 Managing Anxiety in High-Stakes Situations

When it comes to high-stakes situations, whether it's delivering a pivotal presentation, navigating crucial meetings, or facing looming deadlines, anxiety can feel like an unwelcome guest that just won't take the hint to leave. Anxiety, especially in these moments, can be more than just nerve-wracking—it can feel like it's holding your confidence hostage. But imagine if you had a toolbox, one filled with strategies and techniques that could not just quiet that anxiety but also give you a sense of command during these pressure-cooker moments. Let's unpack this toolkit together, starting with identifying what lights the fuse of your anxiety in high-stakes situations.

The first step to managing your anxiety is knowing what exactly triggers it. This is deeply personal and can vary widely. For some, it might be the fear of public speaking; for others, it could be the pressure of delivering to tight deadlines. Start by keeping an anxiety journal. Every time you feel anxious, jot down the situation, the thoughts running through your mind, and how you reacted. Over time, patterns will emerge. You'll start to see which situations crank up your anxiety dial, giving you clearer targets for intervention.

Now, onto preparation, your secret weapon against anxiety. It's like doing a series of stretches before a sprint. Your muscles are prepped, and the chances of a strain are reduced. Let's talk visualization—a technique used by athletes and public speakers alike. Spend a few minutes each day leading up to the event, visualizing yourself succeeding. Picture yourself in the meeting room, feeling calm, delivering your points clearly, and handling questions with ease. This mental rehearsal primes your brain to handle the real event more confidently.

Detailed planning and rehearsal are just as crucial. Break down your tasks into manageable steps and set a timeline. If it's a presentation, script it out and practice till the words feel like old friends. Rehearsal dilutes the fear of the unknown, which is often at the heart of anxiety. And don't forget about setting up contingency plans. Have backups ready—whether it's extra data to support your points or alternative tech setups for your presentation. Knowing you have a plan B can significantly dial down the anxiety.

But what about those moments when, despite all your preparation, anxiety still flares up? Here's where immediate anxiety-reduction techniques come into play. The '5-4-3-2-1' grounding technique is a powerful tool. Notice five things you can see, four things you can touch, three things you can hear, two things you can smell, and one thing you can taste. This technique brings your focus back to the present, cutting through the noise of anxiety. Progressive muscle relaxation is another great tactic. Tense and then relax each muscle group in your body, starting from your toes and working your way up. This physical relaxation can help ease the mental tension as well.

Lastly, let's construct your personalized anxiety response plan. This plan is your playbook for those times when anxiety tries to take center stage. It outlines the steps you'll take to manage your anxiety, tailored to the specific triggers and situations you face. It might include a sequence of actions like taking a two-minute break to practice breathing exercises, using positive self-talk to challenge negative thoughts, or even reaching out to a trusted colleague for a quick pep talk. Having this plan in place ensures you're not just reacting to anxiety but responding to it in a prepared, effective manner.

By building and regularly updating this toolkit, you're not just equipping yourself to handle anxiety in high-stakes situations; you're also transforming your relationship with these pressures. Instead of daunting ordeals, they become stages where you can demonstrate your resilience and capability. With each application of these strategies, you'll find yourself stepping into high-stress scenarios with increasing confidence, not just ready to manage anxiety but to master the moment, no matter the stakes.

4.4 Using Physical Exercise to Manage Emotional Stress

Imagine you could take a magic pill that reduces stress, boosts your mood, sharpens your mind, and to top it off, keeps you fit. Sounds too good to be true? Well, no pill can do all that, but physical exercise comes incredibly close, especially for those of us navigating the choppy waters of ADHD. It's not just about building muscles or endurance; it's about crafting a stronger, more resilient mindset that turns the chaos of ADHD into a symphony of coordinated thoughts and emotions.

Physical exercise, a true ally for the ADHD brain, does more than just pump your heart. It pumps up your mood, thanks to the rush of endorphins, often dubbed as the body's natural feel-good chemicals. For those of us whose brains sometimes spin like a merry-go-round, exercise provides a much-needed pause button. It helps in reducing stress by metabolizing excess stress hormones, like cortisol, clearing your mind to make way for more focused thought processes. Additionally, engaging in regular physical activity has been shown to enhance cognitive functions—it sharpens our memory, improves our concentration, and can even boost our creativity. It's like oiling the cogs of your brain to keep them turning smoothly.

Now, let's dive into the types of exercise that mesh well with ADHD needs. Interval training, for instance, is a perfect fit. This involves short bursts of high-intensity exercise followed by periods of rest or lower-intensity activity. It's dynamic, it's fast-paced, and it mirrors the natural energy ebbs and flows of an ADHD brain, keeping you engaged and not bored. Then there's martial arts—beyond the physical exertion, it demands mental discipline and focus, teaching you to harness your impulsivity into controlled, deliberate movements. And let's not forget about yoga—a practice that combines physical movement with mindful breathing, promoting both physical and mental relaxation, helping to control that often-frenetic ADHD energy.

Incorporating these activities into your hectic schedule might seem daunting, but it's all about weaving them into your daily routine in manageable doses. Think micro workouts—short 10–15-minute intervals where you engage in quick, intense activities like jump rope or a set of burpees. These can be slotted into your morning routine, your lunch break, or even during those few minutes you usually spend scrolling through emails. The key is consistency rather than intensity. It's not about how hard you push in a single session, but about making exercise a regular part of your life.

When it comes to setting realistic exercise goals, think small steps leading to big changes. Start with what feels doable—maybe it's walking for 15 minutes a day or doing yoga every other morning. Set goals that are specific, measurable, attainable, relevant, and time-bound (SMART). Perhaps your goal is to attend three yoga classes per week for a month. By framing your goals this way, they become less daunting and more of a structured path you can confidently walk down.

Monitoring your progress is crucial. It's not just about tracking how many minutes you ran or how many yoga poses you mastered; it's about observing how exercise impacts your stress levels and emotional state. Keep a simple log where you jot down your daily activity and note any changes in how you feel. Are you sleeping better? Is it easier to concentrate after a run? This log will not only keep you motivated but also help you tweak your routine as you discover what works best for your unique ADHD profile.

Exercise, in the grand symphony of ADHD management strategies, is like the steady beat of a drum, providing rhythm and structure to our often-chaotic experiences. It strengthens not just our bodies but our minds, giving us the clarity and calm needed to navigate life's challenges more effectively. As you lace up your sneakers and step onto the track, remember that each step is a step towards not just better physical health, but a more balanced, focused, and joyful life.

As we wrap up this chapter on managing stress and emotional regulation, we've journeyed through mindfulness, cognitive behavioral techniques, handling anxiety, and the power of physical exercise. Each strategy offers unique benefits and, when combined, can provide a robust framework for not just coping with ADHD but thriving despite it.

But let's keep it real: the goal isn't to eliminate stress or anxiety completely—because, come on, life without its ups and downs would be like a Kevin Hart movie without a single laugh. Boring! Instead, it's about managing these experiences so they don't mess with your flow. Think of it as becoming a stress ninja, dodging anxiety attacks like you're in an action flick, with a few epic moves and a whole lot of swagger.

Now, picture this: you, strutting forward, tools in hand, ready to face life's challenges like you're about to drop the hottest album of the year. We're talking resilience, strategy, and a touch of grace. And you better not forget the humor! Laughter is like that secret sauce that makes everything better. So, get ready to tackle life's rollercoaster with a toolkit that's as versatile as a Swiss Army knife and as powerful as a superhero's utility belt. We got this; Let's go!

Key Takeaways

4.1 Mindfulness Practices for Stress Reduction

- **Introduction to Mindfulness:** Mindfulness involves being present and fully engaged in the moment, helping ADHD brains manage stress and emotions by observing thoughts without judgment.
- **Simple Mindfulness Exercises:**

- **Breathing Techniques:** Use the "4-7-8" method to slow down and refocus.
- **Mindful Listening:** Concentrate fully on the speaker to enhance interactions.
- **Mindful Walking:** Take deliberate, slow walks to clear your mind and reset.

- **Integrating Mindfulness:** Incorporate short mindfulness sessions into daily routines, use mindfulness cues before important tasks, and keep a mindfulness journal to track progress.
- **Resources:**

- **Apps:** Headspace, Insight Timer
- **Books:** "Wherever You Go, There You Are" by Jon Kabat-Zinn

4.2 Cognitive Behavioral Techniques for Emotional Control

- **Introduction to CBT:** CBT helps understand and change the connection between thoughts, emotions, and behaviors, useful for addressing negative thinking patterns common in ADHD.
- **Cognitive Restructuring:** Challenge irrational beliefs by examining evidence for and against them.
- **Thought Records:** Keep a diary of stressful situations, thoughts, and emotions to identify patterns and change reactions.
- **Role-Playing:** Practice handling stressful scenarios to rehearse healthy responses.
- **CBT Toolkit:** Include key phrases, reminder cards, and step-by-step guides for cognitive restructuring and thought recording.

4.3 Managing Anxiety in High-Stakes Situations

- **Identifying Triggers:** Keep an anxiety journal to identify situations that trigger anxiety.
- **Preparation:**
- **Visualization:** Mentally rehearse success in high-stakes scenarios.

- **Detailed Planning and Rehearsal:** Break tasks into manageable steps, practice, and set contingency plans.
- **Immediate Anxiety-Reduction Techniques:**
- **5-4-3-2-1 Grounding Technique:** Use sensory observations to refocus.
- **Progressive Muscle Relaxation:** Tense and relax each muscle group to ease mental tension.
- **Personalized Anxiety Response Plan:** Outline steps to manage anxiety, including breathing exercises, positive self-talk, and reaching out for support.

4.4 Using Physical Exercise to Manage Emotional Stress

- **Benefits of Exercise:** Reduces stress, boosts mood, enhances cognitive functions, and provides a break from mental chaos.
- **Types of Exercise:**
- **Interval Training:** Short bursts of high-intensity exercise followed by rest.
- **Martial Arts:** Combines physical exertion with mental discipline.
- **Yoga:** Combines physical movement with mindful breathing for relaxation.

- **Incorporating Exercise:** Use micro workouts, set realistic goals, and maintain consistency.
- **Monitoring Progress:** Keep a log of exercise activities and observe changes in stress levels and emotional state.

Chapter 5:

Leveraging ADHD Strengths in Careers

"Being dyslexic and having ADHD, I think I've been able to see the world in a slightly different way to most people."

- Sir Richard Branson

Have you ever found yourself so engrossed in a project that the world around you seems to fade away, leaving nothing but you and your work dancing in a perfect rhythm? This intense focus, often referred to as hyperfocus, is a common trait of ADHD. While it's often painted in a negative light, suggesting we can't control our attention, what if we flipped the script? What if we viewed this ability as a supercharged engine that, when properly managed, can propel us toward incredible achievements in our careers? Let's dive into understanding hyperfocus and how you can channel this unique aspect of ADHD to your advantage in the professional realm.

5.1 Channeling Hyperfocus for Career Advancement

Understanding Hyperfocus

Hyperfocus, the ability to become deeply engrossed in tasks that are stimulating and rewarding, is like having a secret weapon in your ADHD arsenal. This state can be so absorbing that it might feel like the world has melted away, leaving only you and the task at hand. It's a double-edged sword, though. On one side, it can lead to remarkable productivity and creativity, allowing you to accomplish tasks in a flow state that others might find impossible. On the other, without proper management, it can lead to missed deadlines on other projects or neglected responsibilities.

However, when directed effectively, hyperfocus becomes an incredible asset. It allows you to delve deeply into complex problems, powering through challenges with a laser-like concentration that few can match. This can be especially valuable in careers where innovation, problem-solving, and intensive focus are key to success.

Identifying Opportunities for Hyperfocus

To harness this power, start by identifying tasks and projects in your career that genuinely excite and engage you. These are the tasks where hyperfocus can naturally take the lead. They might be complex data analysis for a business strategist, creative design work for a marketer, or detailed research for a developer.

The trick is to align these tasks with critical business outcomes. When your hyper focused efforts directly contribute to key goals or projects, your work doesn't just stay busy; it becomes impactful. For instance, if you're in a tech company, you might hyperfocus on streamlining user experience or developing a feature that enhances product functionality. This not only makes your work satisfying but also highly visible and valuable to your team and company.

Managing Hyperfocus

Managing hyperfocus involves creating an environment where this trait can be a boom, not a bam. This includes setting timers to remind you to take breaks and check in on other responsibilities, scheduling hyperfocus sessions during times when you're least likely to be interrupted, and using reminders for transitions.

Tools like time-blocking apps can be particularly helpful. They allow you to allocate specific times for deep focus work, reminding you to shift gears when necessary. This helps in maintaining a balance, ensuring that while you capitalize on your ability to hyperfocus, you're not overlooking other essential tasks or meetings.

Leveraging Hyperfocus in Teams

Communicating your hyperfocus tendencies to your team and managers is crucial. It involves letting them know about your unique working style and how it can sometimes lead to periods where you're deeply engrossed in a task. This transparency helps in setting the right expectations and allows your team to better support you.

Moreover, when they understand that this trait can lead to high-quality work, they're more likely to see it as an asset. You can also discuss structuring your responsibilities to include tasks that benefit significantly from deep focus, making your ADHD a direct contributor to team success. This not only improves team dynamics but also ensures that you are seen as a valuable, integral member of the team, whose unique capabilities bring essential benefits to collective efforts.

By understanding, managing, and communicating about your hyperfocus, you transform this trait from a potential hurdle into a profound strength. It becomes a key player in your career advancement, allowing you to deliver exceptional results and stand out in your professional landscape. Embrace this focus, guide it with intention, and watch as it accelerates your journey up the career ladder, turning tasks into triumphs and goals into achievements.

5.2 Creative Problem-Solving with ADHD

Oh!...the wild, wacky world of ADHD where the brain is less like well-filed libraries and more like pinball machines—thoughts pinging and ideas zinging from bumper to bumper. It's this very whirlwind of thought, this capacity for divergent thinking, that not only sparks creativity but can ignite some truly innovative problem-solving. Divergent thinking, you see, is our ability to think more broadly and to generate a range of solutions around a single topic, which is kind of our superpower. This trait allows us to see connections where others might see dead ends, making us natural innovators at heart.

Now, fostering a creative work environment that really lets this kind of thinking thrive can be a game-changer. Imagine a workplace that not only understands the ADHD mind but celebrates it. This starts with flexibility—flexible hours, flexible workspaces, and even flexible job roles. Such an environment acknowledges that creativity doesn't always operate on a 9-to-5 schedule. Sometimes our best ideas come at the crack of dawn, or in the quiet after everyone else has logged off.

Then, there's the setup of creativity sessions. These are designated times or spaces where wild ideas are not just allowed but encouraged. Think of it as a sandbox for grown-ups. No idea is too outlandish, no solution too out there. It's about brainstorming in its purest form. In such sessions, the usual rules are paused, and the floor is open to all sorts of thoughts and perspectives. This can be particularly liberating for someone with ADHD, as it harnesses our natural inclination to leapfrog from idea to idea.

Techniques like mind mapping or reverse thinking can also be incredibly effective in a creative work setting. Mind mapping allows us to visually plot out our thoughts, which can be particularly helpful when our brains are overflowing with ideas. It turns the chaos into a roadmap, making it easier to explore connections and expand on concepts. Reverse thinking, on the other hand, flips problems on their head. Start with the desired outcome and work backwards to figure out how to achieve it. It's a fun way to tackle challenges and can often lead to more innovative solutions.

Case Studies of Innovation

To see these principles in action, let's zoom in on a few real-world warriors who have harnessed their ADHD to bring valuable innovations to their workplaces.

Take, for instance, a tech developer named Alex. Known for his whirlwind brainstorms, Alex utilized mind mapping to develop a new app feature that significantly improved user engagement. His ability to see the "big picture" allowed him to connect user feedback with innovative tech solutions, simplifying a complex problem into a user-friendly feature.

Then there's Priya, a marketing strategist with a knack for reverse thinking. Faced with a campaign that needed a major boost, she started with her desired spike in customer engagement and worked backwards to reengineer the campaign's weaker spots. Her approach not only turned the campaign around but also set new benchmarks for future projects.

Last, Dr. Raj's, a medical surgeon, who struggled with ADHD in his early career to becoming a leading surgeon in his field. He understood he had an ability to think creatively which played a crucial role in performing intricate surgical procedures.

These cases underline not just the potential but the real-world applicability of ADHD-driven creativity in solving work-related problems. Each example showcases how thinking differently, a natural trait for many of us with ADHD, isn't just about having unique ideas but about transforming these ideas into practical solutions that drive business success.

So, if you've ever felt out of step because your brain goes off on tangents or sees rainbows where others see rain, remember that in the right environment, with strategies that play to your strengths, your creative problem-solving isn't just a quirk—it's your superpower. Whether you're sketching out mind maps, flipping problems on their head, or brainstorming up a storm, your unique approach is not just valuable; it's indispensable. It's what keeps the wheels of innovation turning, pushing the boundaries of what's possible in your career and beyond.

5.3 Turning Impulsivity into Quick Decision-Making

When most folks hear "impulsivity," their minds might dart straight to reckless decisions and unchecked actions, the kind that can lead to face-palm moments. But hey, let's spin that narrative a bit, shall we? Imagine impulsivity not as your frenemy, but as a kind of secret sauce for rapid, dynamic decision-making. Yes, you heard that right. In the high-speed freeway of professional life, where decisions often need to be made yesterday, your natural impulsiveness can actually be your ally—if you know how to channel it right.

Reframing Impulsivity

So, let's redefine impulsivity. Instead of seeing it as a rush towards action without thought, think of it as the ability to make swift decisions, a trait that can be incredibly valuable in fast-paced environments. Think about a stock trader, for instance. In the buzzing world of stocks, decisions often need to be made in seconds, not minutes. Here, the ability to act swiftly can mean the difference between capitalizing on an opportunity or missing out. Similarly, in creative fields like advertising or media, being able to quickly generate and respond to ideas can keep you steps ahead of the competition. This doesn't just apply to high-stakes trading or brainstorming sessions; it's relevant in everyday work scenarios that require quick thinking and adaptability.

Controlled Risk-Taking

Now, the trick is to marry impulsivity with strategy, transforming raw speed into controlled agility. Structured risk-taking allows you to make quick decisions with a safety net. For instance, set boundaries for decisions that need speedy action versus those that require more thought. A simple method could be categorizing decisions into low, medium, and high impact. Low-impact decisions, like choosing the format for a presentation, can be made quickly, relying on your impulsive strengths. High-impact decisions, like approving a project budget, might need a pause and a more thorough evaluation.

Another strategy is to establish a 'risk threshold'. This is like setting a speed limit for your decision-making. Determine in advance the level of risk you are comfortable taking without needing to hit the brakes for a detailed analysis. This allows you to make quick decisions confidently within a defined safe zone, reducing the likelihood of significant negative consequences.

Training for Quick Decision Making

Training your impulsivity for precision decision-making can be likened to tuning a sports car: you want the speed, but you need control just as much. Scenario planning is a fantastic way to practice. This involves walking through different decision-making scenarios and planning out your actions. For example, if you're in marketing, you might run through scenarios like an unexpected PR crisis or a sudden opportunity to launch a new campaign. What would you do first? What's the immediate action, and what requires more planning?

Decision-making exercises also hone your ability to think on your feet. Set up regular drills that mimic real-life challenges where you must make decisions quickly. You could use business simulations, role-playing, or even computer games designed to improve cognitive flexibility and speed. The goal is to train your brain to make rapid decisions effectively and responsibly, turning natural impulsivity into a refined skill.

Balancing Impulsivity with Caution

Finally, balancing the scales between impulsivity and caution is key. Here's where the 'pause and plan' technique becomes invaluable. Before making a decision, take a brief moment, maybe just a few seconds, to assess the situation. Ask yourself: What's the worst that could happen? Do I have all the information I need? This brief pause can be enough to add a layer of reflection to your decision-making process, ensuring that your actions are both swift and smart.

Incorporating simple checks like these helps maintain a balance where you leverage the speed of your impulsivity but temper it with strategic pauses. This approach ensures that your decisions are not just fast but also forward-thinking, aligning quick action with long-term goals. By refining your impulsivity in this way, you turn what many perceive as a professional hurdle into a distinct competitive edge, allowing you to navigate the rapid currents of your career with both speed and intent.

As we continue to explore the multifaceted implications of ADHD traits in professional settings, remember that each trait, each nuance of your cognitive style, holds potential. It's not about changing who you are but about understanding and directing your innate tendencies in ways that propel you forward. In your hands, impulsivity is not a flaw but a powerful tool, ready to be mastered and wielded with precision in the relentless pursuit of your career aspirations.

5.4 Resilience and Adaptability as Career Strengths

Think of resilience as the psychological muscle that's flexed and toned through the everyday hustle of managing ADHD. It's not just about bouncing back; it's about springing forward, armed with lessons learned from each challenge. Living with ADHD means constantly navigating a maze of distractions, hyperactivity, and the social stigmas that tag along. This relentless navigation doesn't just build character; it builds resilience. You learn to adapt, to adjust, and to accommodate not just to survive but to thrive. Each day presents a new set of challenges, and each challenge is an opportunity to develop this crucial skill.

Now, how can you take this inherent resilience and crank it up a notch? Start by cultivating a growth mindset—the belief that abilities can be developed through dedication and hard work. This mindset is particularly powerful for professionals with ADHD because it shifts our focus from what we can't do to what we can achieve through effort and learning. Engage in reflective practices like journaling about your daily experiences, focusing on what went well and what you could improve. This not only helps in processing the day's events but also in recognizing and celebrating your small victories—essential fuel for building resilience.

Seeking feedback is another strategy that can significantly enhance your resilience. It might feel daunting, especially when your ADHD traits are often seen under a critical light. However, constructive feedback is invaluable as it provides insights not just into your performance but also into how you can leverage your strengths more effectively. Approach feedback with an open mind and a clear goal of learning and growth. Remember, every piece of feedback is a stepping stone to betterment, not a judgement of your worth.

Adaptability, on the other hand, is your ability to adjust to new conditions—a skill where individuals with ADHD naturally excel. In the fast-paced modern workplace, where change is the only constant, adaptability is a prized asset. Your innate ability to pivot quickly in response to changing circumstances is not just about staying afloat; it's about being able to dance in the rain while others are still searching for an umbrella.

In environments that value agility, your natural adaptability allows you to embrace and lead change rather than resist it. Whether it's a sudden shift in project direction, a new software tool, or a complete overhaul of strategy, you can navigate these changes with more ease than most. This agility makes you an invaluable asset to any team, particularly in industries where the ability to pivot quickly and effectively is key to success.

Let's illustrate this with a couple of stories from the trenches. Consider Maya, a project manager in a tech startup, known for her ADHD-driven energy and adaptability. When her company decided to pivot from web-based to mobile-first services, Maya took the lead in managing the transition. Her ability to think on her feet and her openness to exploring new strategies led to a seamless integration of the new services, significantly boosting the company's performance and customer satisfaction.

Then there's Jamal, a graphic designer with a flair for adapting on the fly. Faced with a major client's feedback that called for a complete redesign of a campaign just days before launch, Jamal's flexible thinking and creative agility allowed him to overhaul the design overnight. The campaign turned out to be one of the agency's most successful, with the client praising the quick turnaround and innovative approach.

These stories underscore the power of adaptability—not just as a survival mechanism but as a strategic asset that can lead to substantial career advancements and successes. Your ability to adapt isn't just about dealing with the cards you're dealt; it's about reshuffling the deck and finding new ways to win the game.

As we wrap up this exploration of resilience and adaptability, remember that these aren't just skills but superpowers that can dramatically enhance your professional life. They transform challenges into opportunities and uncertainties into adventures. Embrace these strengths, develop them with intention, and watch as they open new doors in your career, allowing you to meet the future with confidence and curiosity.Moving forward, let's continue to explore how leveraging your unique ADHD traits can not only enhance your career but also contribute to a richer, more fulfilling professional journey.

Key Takeaways

5.1 Channeling Hyperfocus for Career Advancement

- **Understanding Hyperfocus:** Hyperfocus is the intense concentration on tasks that are stimulating and rewarding, which can lead to remarkable productivity and creativity.
- **Identifying Opportunities:** Find tasks and projects that genuinely excite you and align with critical business outcomes to naturally engage hyperfocus.
- **Managing Hyperfocus:** Set timers for breaks, schedule hyperfocus sessions during low-interruption times, and use time-blocking apps to balance deep focus with other responsibilities.
- **Leveraging in Teams:** Communicate your working style to your team and managers, allowing them to support and appreciate your deep focus on high-value tasks.

5.2 Creative Problem-Solving with ADHD

- **Divergent Thinking:** ADHD fosters divergent thinking, allowing for broader and more creative solutions.
- **Fostering a Creative Environment:** Encourage flexibility in hours, workspaces, and job roles, and create designated creativity sessions.
- **Techniques:** Use mind mapping for visual idea plotting and reverse thinking to explore innovative solutions.
- **Case Studies:** Real-world examples (e.g., tech developer, marketing strategist) show how ADHD-driven creativity leads to significant professional achievements.

5.3 Turning Impulsivity into Quick Decision-Making

- **Reframing Impulsivity:** View impulsivity as an ability to make swift decisions, valuable in fast-paced environments.
- **Controlled Risk-Taking:** Establish boundaries for quick decisions and set a risk threshold for safe decision-making.

- **Training Techniques:** Practice scenario planning and decision-making exercises to refine rapid decision-making skills.
- **Balancing Impulsivity:** Use the 'pause and plan' technique to add a layer of reflection, ensuring decisions are both swift and smart.

5.4 Resilience and Adaptability as Career Strengths

- **Building Resilience:** Cultivate a growth mindset, engage in reflective practices, and seek constructive feedback.
- **Embracing Adaptability:** Leverage the natural ability to pivot quickly in response to changing circumstances, making you invaluable in agile environments.
- **Real-World Examples:** Stories of professionals (e.g., project manager, graphic designer) who used adaptability to lead successful changes and achieve career milestones.
- **Strategic Asset:** Adaptability transforms challenges into opportunities and is key to thriving in dynamic workplaces.

******Make a Difference with Your Review******
Unlock the Power of Generosity

"Acts of kindness are a way to make the world a happier place." - Unknown

Have you ever felt like a circus juggler with one too many flaming torches in the air, desperately trying not to get burned? That's daily life for many people with ADHD, right? Time management might seem like a mythical beast we've all heard of but never actually seen. But here's the good news: it's not only real, it can actually be tamed and turned into one of your best allies.

People who give without expectation live longer, happier lives and make more money. So if we've got a shot at that during our time together, darn it, I'm going to try.

To make that happen, I have a question for you...

Would you help someone you've never met, even if you never got credit for it?

Who is this person you ask? They are like you. Or, at least, like you used to be. Less experienced, wanting to make a difference, and needing help, but not sure where to look.

My mission is to make **Navigating ADHD For Adults: 12 Proven Strategies and Techniques to Harness your ADHD in Relationships, Work, and at Home** to everyone. Everything I do stems from that mission. And, the only way for me to accomplish that mission is by reaching...well...everyone.

This is where you come in. Most people do, in fact, judge a book by its cover (and its reviews). So here's my ask on behalf of a struggling ADHD professional you've never met:

Please help that ADHD Professional by leaving this book a review.

Your gift costs no money and less than 60 seconds to make a real difference, but can change a fellow ADHD Professional's life forever. Your review could help...

...one more small business provide for their community. ...one more entrepreneur support their family. ...one more employee get meaningful work. ...one more client transform their life. ...one more dream come true. To get that 'feel good' feeling and help this person for real, all you have to do is...and it takes less than 60 seconds... leave a review.

Simply scan the QR code below to leave your review:

If you feel good about helping a faceless ADHD Professional, you are my kind of person. Welcome to the club. You're one of us. I'm that much more excited to help you **comprehend, dominate, and excel in your career** easier than you can possibly imagine.

You'll love the **strategies** I'm about to share in the coming chapters.

Thank you from the bottom of my heart. Now, back to our regularly scheduled program-ming.

- Your biggest fan, **Phoenix J. Waldren**

PS - Fun fact: If you provide something of value to another person, it makes you more valuable to them. If you'd like goodwill straight from another professional - and you believe this book will help them - send this book their way.

Chapter 6:

Multitasking and Workload Management

"Focus is about saying no. You've got to say no, no, no. When you say no, you piss off people. But the only way to get your priorities straight is by saying no."

- Steve Jobs

Imagine you're a DJ at the hottest club in town—not just spinning tracks but also managing the lights, the crowd, and maybe even the bar. That's a lot like managing a day with ADHD, trying to keep the beats of your tasks, responsibilities, and deadlines all syncing perfectly without letting one track drown out the others. It's a wild ride, right? And while this might paint a picture of chaos, there's a method to this madness, which starts with the art of prioritization—a skill as crucial as the ability to find that perfect song that keeps the energy flowing.

6.1 Prioritization Frameworks for the ADHD Mind

Introduction to Prioritization

Prioritization is your secret weapon, the DJ's mixer that allows you to adjust the volume of life's tracks to ensure everything plays harmoniously. For professionals with ADHD, where every task can seem equally urgent, learning to prioritize effectively isn't just helpful; it's essential. It's about knowing which tasks to turn up, which to turn down, and which to pause altogether. This doesn't just help in managing the workload; it helps in reducing the overwhelm that can come from a to-do list that feels like it's set on shuffle.

Effective Prioritization Techniques

Let's dive into some techniques that can turn the cacophony of tasks into a well-orchestrated symphony. First up, the Eisenhower Box, also known as the urgent-important matrix. Picture a simple grid with four quadrants: urgent and important, important but not urgent, urgent but not important, and neither urgent nor important. This visual tool helps you quickly categorize your tasks and decide which need your immediate attention, which should be scheduled, which can be delegated, and which (let's be honest) can be dropped.

Then there's the ABC prioritization technique, which is like creating a playlist for your day. 'A' tasks are your must-dos—these are your headliners, the big acts that can make or break your day. 'B' tasks are important but can wait if need be—they're your opening acts, setting the stage but not the main show. 'C' tasks? Those are your nice-to-dos, like the after-party—it's great if you can get to them, but no stress if not. By categorizing tasks this way, you can manage your energy and focus where it counts, ensuring you're always playing the right tunes at the right time.

Daily Prioritization Practice

Making prioritization a daily practice is like setting up your playlist before the club opens. Each morning, take a few minutes to list your tasks and run them through the Eisenhower Box or the ABC technique. This not only sets the tone for your day but also puts you in control, allowing you to manage your tasks rather than letting them manage you. Stay flexible—new tasks will pop up, and priorities might shift. The key is to adjust your 'playlist' as needed without losing the beat.

Tools and Apps to Aid Prioritization

In our digital age, several tools can help keep your prioritization clear and visible. Task management apps like Asana or Trello are like your DJ software, allowing you to organize, label, and rearrange your tasks with ease. These tools often offer features that let you color-code tasks or set reminders, making it easy to see at a glance what needs your attention. Integrating these apps into your daily routine can be a game-changer, ensuring your tasks are not just organized but also aligned with your energy levels and focus throughout the day.

Interactive Element: Task Management App Exploration

To truly integrate these prioritization techniques into your life, why not take a moment to explore some task management apps? Here's a simple exercise: download a task management app like Todoist or Trello, and spend a few minutes setting up your tasks for the next day using the ABC technique. Use color coding or labels to differentiate between A, B, and C tasks. Notice how visualizing your tasks this way can change your perspective on what's truly important, and reflect on how this might help in reducing feelings of overwhelm.

By mastering these prioritization frameworks, you not only streamline your workload but also enhance your overall productivity and well-being. It's about making each day less about firefighting and more about strategically managing your energy across tasks that truly move the needle in your life and career. So, let's turn down the volume on the non-essentials, crank up the focus on what really matters, and get ready to rock the decks of your day with confidence and control.

6.2 Setting Clear Boundaries Between Tasks

Let's chat about the art of setting boundaries between tasks, a must-have skill for us in the ADHD tribe. Think of each task as a different act in a circus—you wouldn't want the clowns barging in on the tightrope walkers, right? That's pretty much what happens when tasks bleed into one another without clear boundaries. This overlap isn't just a recipe for confusion; it cranks up stress levels and tramples on productivity, leaving us feeling like we've been in a tussle with a tornado. Establishing clear task boundaries is like giving each circus act its own spotlight moment, ensuring everything runs smoothly and nothing gets more attention than it should.

Now, onto some nifty techniques for drawing those lines in the sand—or in our case, the office. Time blocking is a super tool here. It's all about dedicating specific chunks of time to specific tasks. Imagine you're creating a playlist for your day; each song is a task, and it plays for a set amount of time before the next tune kicks in. This method not only keeps you on track with each task but also minimizes the risk of tasks morphing into one endless, confusing medley. You could start with blocking out morning hours for deep-focus work and save the afternoons for meetings and emails. It's like planning your day in high-definition, where you see the boundaries clearly and stick to them.

Using physical or digital signals can also help cement these boundaries. For instance, if you're working on two different projects, use separate notebooks or folders for each—red for project A, blue for project B. Digitally, you could use different desktops or browser profiles for various tasks. Tools like virtual desktops on your computer can be lifesavers, allowing you to switch between tasks without losing your place. Think of these as your virtual rooms, each holding a different part of your work life. When you enter one, you're fully there, and when it's time to switch, you leave everything behind, ready to embrace the next task fully.

But what about those days when your environment feels about as predictable as a plot twist in a mystery novel? Maintaining task boundaries when your workday throws you curveballs requires a blend of firmness and flexibility. Communicating your needs clearly to your colleagues and superiors is key. Let them know when you're in a time-blocked zone and when you're available. Visual cues can help here too—a closed door or a headphone on can signal to others that you're deep in focus. And when interruptions do happen, as they inevitably will, having a quick method to jot down where you left off before switching tasks can help reduce the friction and ease your return later.

The psychological perks of well-defined task boundaries are like a balm for the ADHD soul. There's a profound sense of control and accomplishment that comes from ticking off tasks within their set boundaries. This not only boosts satisfaction but also dials down the chaos, making the task juggle feel less like a frantic scramble and more like a well-choreographed dance. Each task gets its moment in the sun, and you get to enjoy a clearer headspace and a more productive day.

So, as you move through your workweek, think of yourself as both the choreographer and the performer in your own productivity ballet. By setting and respecting clear boundaries between your tasks, you're choreographing a performance where both your satisfaction and your output get a standing ovation. Remember, in the grand show of your professional life, how you arrange and respect your tasks can make all the difference between a blockbuster hit and a box office flop.

6.3 Focus Blocks: Single-Tasking in a Multitasking World

Ah, multitasking, the modern-day badge of honor that so many of us wear with pride. It's like spinning several plates while balancing on a unicycle—impressive, sure, but is it really the best way to get things done? Let's bust a myth right here: while multitasking might make you feel like a productivity superhero, studies suggest it's more likely to be your kryptonite, especially if you're juggling ADHD alongside those metaphorical plates.

For professionals with ADHD, multitasking can scatter our already sprinting thoughts even further, turning what should be a manageable workload into a chaotic flurry of half-completed tasks. Enter the concept of focus blocks—our secret weapon against the multitasking mayhem. Imagine setting aside chunks of time where your world shrinks down to just one task. No distractions, no switching gears—just you and the task at hand. It's not just about working hard; it's about working smart, giving one task your undivided attention until it's done or until the block ends.

Creating these focus blocks might sound like a walk in the park, but there's an art to it. First, consider the length of these blocks. You might think that longer is better, but remember, ADHD brains do a fantastic dance of sprint and rest. Typically, 25-30 minutes of focused time followed by a 5-minute break can work wonders. These mini-breaks are crucial—they give your brain a moment to breathe, reducing the risk of cognitive overload and keeping your motivation fresh.

Scheduling these blocks can be just as important as their duration. Try to align them with the times of day when you feel most energized and alert. Maybe you're a morning person, where your focus peaks with the sunrise. Or perhaps you find your stride later in the day. By aligning your focus blocks with your natural energy fluctuations, you amplify their effectiveness, turning peak times into peak productivity.

Now, let's tailor these blocks to fit the unique contours of your ADHD. Incorporating short breaks within these focus periods can help manage the restlessness that often accompanies our condition. Use these breaks for quick physical activities like stretching or a brisk walk—anything that helps to reset your attention without leading you down a rabbit hole of distraction. Additionally, consider layering in some motivational rewards. Finished a focus block without straying? Treat yourself to a small reward—maybe a cup of your favorite coffee or a few minutes with a book. These little incentives can boost your motivation and make the focus block something you look forward to.

Tools to Enhance Focus During These Blocks

Equipping yourself with the right tools can transform your focus blocks from a good idea to a great practice. Let's start with ambient noise apps. Whether it's the soothing sounds of rain or the gentle hum of a coffee shop, ambient noise can drown out the jarring silence that sometimes amplifies internal distractions. Apps like Noisli or A Soft Murmur offer customizable soundscapes that can help keep your mind engaged and less prone to wander.

For those of us who find music more focusing than noise, consider creating a focus-enhancing playlist. The key here is to choose music that energizes without distracting. Instrumental tracks or classical music can be great choices, providing a rhythmic backdrop that improves concentration without pulling your mind away with lyrics or complex compositions.

Then there are distraction blockers—digital lifesavers for when the internet beckons with its siren call of social media and endless scrolling. Tools like Freedom or Cold Turkey allow you to block distracting websites or apps during your focus blocks, ensuring that your digital environment is as clutter-free as your mental one.

By embracing the concept of focus blocks and equipping yourself with these focus-enhancing tools, you're not just committing to more productive work sessions; you're also taking a stand against the myth that multitasking is the only way to work. It's about giving each task the attention it deserves, and in doing so, giving yourself the best chance to succeed and shine in your endeavors, one focused block at a time.

6.4 Delegation Skills for People with ADHD

Let's talk about delegation. The mere thought of handing off tasks can feel like trying to give away a piece of our own puzzle—it just doesn't seem to fit right. Maybe it's the fear that nobody can do it *quite* right, or perhaps it's the worry that letting go means losing control. These feelings are like invisible handcuffs that keep us from sharing responsibilities, ultimately leading to overwork and, let's be honest, an ever-expanding to-do list that could give War and Peace a run for its money in terms of complexity.

First up, overcoming these emotional and psychological barriers is key. Perfectionism is a common guest at our table, often whispering that if something needs to be done right, it has to be done by us. But here's the thing—delegation isn't about offloading work just because; it's about strategic sharing of tasks to enhance efficiency and team capacity. To ease the grip of perfectionism, start small. Delegate tasks that have a little more wiggle room for outcomes. This could be something like organizing files or managing routine updates. As you see others handle these tasks competently, it builds trust, slowly silencing that nagging voice of doubt.

Next, let's lay out the steps to effective delegation. The first step is choosing the right tasks to delegate. Look for tasks that are time-consuming but don't necessarily require your unique skills or expertise. These are your low-hanging fruits, perfect for passing on to capable hands. Then, selecting the right person is crucial. Consider their skills, workload, and even interest in the task. A well-matched task not only ensures it gets done well but also aids in employee development.

Communicating these tasks clearly is the linchpin in this process. Be specific about what the task entails, the expected outcomes, and the deadlines. Clarity prevents confusion and sets the stage for success. It's like giving someone a treasure map where 'X' marks the spot; they'll know exactly where to dig.

Monitoring these tasks without hovering is a delicate dance. Set up regular check-ins based on the complexity and duration of the task. These aren't just about tracking progress; they're opportunities to provide support and feedback, fostering a sense of guidance rather than surveillance. Tools like project management software can be incredibly useful here. Platforms like Asana or Monday.com allow you to see task progress at a glance without needing to micromanage. They're like having a dashboard for your delegations, providing updates without the need for constant oversight.

Leveraging technology in delegation doesn't stop with project management tools. There are numerous digital resources that can streamline this process. Use shared calendars for deadlines and reminders, cloud storage for accessible documents, and even chat apps for quick questions and updates. These tools not only aid in efficient delegation but also help keep everyone on the same page, minimizing misunderstandings and maximizing productivity.

By embracing these delegation strategies, you're not just unloading your plate; you're enhancing your team's cohesion and capability. It's about transforming delegation from a chore into an opportunity, one that allows you to focus on tasks that genuinely need your attention while fostering an environment of trust and growth. So, let go of those invisible handcuffs and start passing those pieces of the puzzle around. You might just find that they fit perfectly, completing the picture more beautifully than you could have done alone.

As we close this chapter on multitasking and workload management, remember, the goal isn't just about getting things done but about doing them more intelligently. Prioritization, setting boundaries, focus blocks, and delegation—these aren't just tools; they are the building blocks for a more productive, less stressful professional life. They allow you to manage not just your tasks but also your energy, turning everyday work from a source of stress into a source of satisfaction. As we move forward, keep these strategies in mind. They are your companions on this journey, ensuring that every step you take is not just forward but upward.

Next, we'll explore strategies for maintaining momentum and motivation, ensuring that your energy and enthusiasm are as sustainable as your workload management. Stay tuned!

Key Takeaways

6.1 Prioritization Frameworks for the ADHD Mind

- **Introduction to Prioritization:** Effective prioritization helps manage workload and reduces overwhelm by focusing on what truly matters.
- **Techniques:**
- **Eisenhower Box:** Categorizes tasks into urgent-important, important-not urgent, urgent-not important, and neither.
- **ABC Prioritization:** 'A' tasks are must-dos, 'B' tasks are important but can wait, and 'C' tasks are nice-to-dos.
- **Daily Practice:** Spend a few minutes each morning prioritizing tasks using these techniques to set a controlled tone for the day.
- **Tools and Apps:** Use task management apps like Asana or Trello to organize, label, and manage tasks visually.

6.2 Setting Clear Boundaries Between Tasks

- **Importance of Boundaries:** Clear boundaries prevent task overlap, reduce stress, and enhance productivity.
- **Techniques:**
- **Time Blocking:** Dedicate specific chunks of time to specific tasks, minimizing the risk of tasks blending together.
- **Physical/Digital Signals:** Use separate notebooks, folders, or virtual desktops for different projects.
- **Environmental Adjustments:** Communicate boundaries to colleagues and use visual cues like closed doors or headphones.
- **Psychological Benefits:** Defined task boundaries create a sense of control and accomplishment.

6.3 Focus Blocks: Single-Tasking in a Multitasking World

- **Concept of Focus Blocks:** Allocate chunks of time to single tasks, avoiding the pitfalls of multitasking.
- **Creating Effective Focus Blocks:**
- **Duration:** Typically 25-30 minutes of focused time followed by a 5-minute break.

- **Scheduling:** Align focus blocks with natural energy peaks.
- **Breaks and Rewards:** Incorporate short breaks and small rewards to maintain motivation.
- **Tools to Enhance Focus:**
- **Ambient Noise Apps:** Use apps like Noisli for customizable soundscapes.
- **Focus Playlists:** Choose instrumental or classical music to maintain concentration.
- **Distraction Blockers:** Use tools like Freedom to block distracting websites.

6.4 Delegation Skills for People with ADHD

- **Overcoming Barriers:** Address perfectionism and fear of losing control to enable effective delegation.
- **Steps for Effective Delegation:**
- **Choose the Right Tasks:** Delegate time-consuming tasks that don't require your unique skills.
- **Select the Right Person:** Match tasks with the appropriate skills and interest.
- **Communicate Clearly:** Provide specific instructions and expected outcomes.
- **Monitor Progress:** Use regular check-ins and project management tools like Asana.

- **Leveraging Technology:** Use shared calendars, cloud storage, and chat apps for efficient delegation and communication.

Chapter 7:

Kickstarting and Sustaining Projects

"All roads that lead to success have to pass through hard work boulevard."

– **Eric Thomas**

Ever stood at the edge of a high dive, toes curled over the edge, heart thumping like a bass drum at a rock concert, only to find yourself unable to jump? That's what kicking off a project can feel like when you're wrestling with ADHD. It's not that you don't want to dive into the cool, refreshing waters of accomplishment—it's just that sometimes, the act of taking that first leap feels overwhelmingly daunting. This, my friends, is what we call initiation paralysis, and it's about as fun as finding a raisin cookie when you expected chocolate chip. Let's unpack this tricky beast, shall we?

7.1 Overcoming Initiation Paralysis

Understanding Initiation Paralysis

Initiation paralysis is like that annoying backseat driver in your brain that keeps saying, "Oh, I wouldn't start yet if I were you." It stems from a cocktail of psychological factors—fear of failure (no one wants to belly flop), overwhelm from unclear task parameters (like diving into murky water), and a classic difficulty in prioritizing (not knowing which diving board to jump from first). For professionals with ADHD, these factors aren't just roadblocks; they're like a traffic jam on the freeway at rush hour.

But here's the kicker: understanding these psychological hold-ups is the first step to overcoming them. Fear of failure often ties into our perfectionist tendencies, making the stakes of starting seem sky-high. Overwhelm creeps in when the scope of the project is as clear as mud. And poor prioritization? It's like having a GPS that can't decide which route is the fastest. Recognizing these triggers helps us map out a more manageable approach to starting projects, turning that paralyzed feeling into a controlled, ready-to-dive posture.

Breaking Tasks into Smaller Steps

Now, you probably heard me say this before but once again, breaking down the high dive into a series of small, padded steps helps significantly. Not so scary anymore, right? Start by breaking them into bite-sized pieces. If it's a report you need to write, break it down: outline, research, write, revise, and polish. Each piece should be small enough to tackle without triggering a fight-or-flight response.

This method reduces the mental load and makes the task seem less daunting. It's like preparing to cook a five-course meal but focusing on one dish at a time. Before you know it, you've got a full spread on the table, and you're not even sweating.

Using External Triggers to Initiate Action

Sometimes, we need a little external nudge to jump-start our engines. This is where setting up external triggers can work wonders. These triggers act as cues to begin a task, pushing us gently off the proverbial diving board. It could be as simple as setting a specific time for task initiation, like programming a phone alarm to signal the start of your writing hour, or establishing a pre-task ritual, like brewing a cup of your favorite coffee before sitting down to work.

These triggers can also be part of your environment. Organize your workspace so that everything you need to start is at arm's reach. Seeing your tools laid out can signal to your brain that it's time to get down to business. Think of it as setting the stage for a performance—the curtain rises, and it's showtime.

Developing a Pre-Task Routine

Speaking of rituals, developing a pre-task routine can be a powerful way to prime your brain for action. This routine should be something that mentally prepares you to dive into your task. Maybe it's a short meditation to clear your mind, a quick physical warm-up to dispel any restlessness, or a review of your goals related to the task at hand, reminding you why you're doing this in the first place.

Your routine should be a Pavlovian signal to your brain: when you do X, it's time to start working on Y. This not only helps in overcoming initiation paralysis but also sets a productive tone for the task ahead, making the transition into work smoother and more natural.

Interactive Element: Goal-Setting Exercise

To put this into practice, let's try a quick exercise. Grab a piece of paper and write down a task you've been putting off. Below it, break it down into three smaller steps. Next to each step, jot down a simple action you can take to make starting easier, like setting a reminder on your phone or preparing your workspace. This exercise isn't just about planning; it's about creating a clear pathway from intention to action.

By tackling initiation paralysis head-on, with a clear understanding of its roots and a toolbox of strategies to overcome it, you're setting yourself up not just to start projects, but to start them with confidence and clarity. Remember, the hardest part of any project is often just starting. Once you're past that, you've cleared the highest hurdle. Now, let's dive in and swim through these projects with the grace of a dolphin and the determination of a shark.

7.2 Maintaining Momentum in Long-Term Projects

Imagine you're on a cross-country road trip. You've got the car all packed, the playlist queued up, and the excitement of the open road before you. But as you hit mile 100, the thrill begins to wane a bit. How do you keep the journey engaging, not just when you're setting off with a full tank and sunny skies, but also when you hit those long stretches of seemingly endless highway? Maintaining momentum in long-term projects is a lot like keeping that road trip lively and interesting, even when you're miles from your destination.

One of the best strategies to keep your project engine running smoothly is to regularly revisit the project's goals and the personal rewards of completing it. This isn't just about reminding yourself what you're working towards, but also why you started in the first place. Maybe you're working on a big presentation that could lead to a promotion, or perhaps it's a personal project that fulfills a passion. Whatever it is, reconnecting with the 'why' can reignite your motivation, much like reminding yourself of the stunning beach waiting at the end of your road trip. Set up regular review sessions—maybe once a week or after every major milestone—to reflect on your progress and realign with your initial excitement.

Flexibility in planning is your co-pilot here. Just as detours and road closures require you to adjust your route without losing sight of your destination, effective project management often requires you to be adaptable in your planning. This means being open to adjusting your methods and timelines based on ongoing progress and any setbacks you encounter. For instance, if a key resource becomes unavailable, instead of sticking rigidly to your original plan, explore alternative solutions that keep the project moving forward. This adaptability not only helps in tackling immediate challenges but also in maintaining a steady pace towards project completion.

Accountability mechanisms are like your trusted GPS, keeping you on track and alerting you if you veer off course. Regular check-ins with a mentor or a peer group provide external perspectives that can enhance your focus and commitment. These sessions serve as checkpoints where you can share progress, set back, and adjust plans. They also create a sense of obligation that can be incredibly motivating. Knowing that you'll need to report on your progress can spur you to keep moving forward, even when the road seems long. Make these check-ins engaging and constructive; they should be something you look forward to, not dread.

Lastly, the journey of any long-term project benefits immensely from regular intervals for reflection and adjustment. This is akin to stopping by a scenic overlook to assess how far you've come and how far you still have to go. Periodically step back from the day-to-day tasks and review the entire project's progress. Are you still on the right path? Have certain assumptions changed? What have you learned, and how can this knowledge improve your approach moving forward? Setting aside time for these reflections allows you to address potential issues before they turn into significant obstacles, ensuring your project stays on a path to success.

By weaving these strategies into the fabric of your project management approach, you not only sustain momentum but also cultivate a deeper engagement with your work. It transforms long-term projects from daunting marathons to exciting journeys, full of opportunities for growth and achievement. So, keep your eyes on the road ahead, adjust your mirrors as needed, and drive your project forward with confidence and clarity.

7.3 Setting and Achieving Short-Term Milestones

Imagine you're on a long hike. The path stretches miles ahead, weaving through mountains and forests. It's beautiful but daunting. Now, picture there are markers along the way, each one representing a manageable stretch of that journey. Reaching each marker gives you a sense of progress and a moment to celebrate, renewing your energy for the next leg. This is exactly why short-term milestones in projects are so critical, especially when navigating the complexities of ADHD. They break down the 'marathon' into a series of 'sprints' that keep your motivation fresh and your spirits high.

Short-term milestones are like mini-goals, points we set along the timeline of a larger project that act as both motivators and indicators of progress. For someone with ADHD, whose time perception might as well have its own quirky time zone, these milestones are invaluable. They provide a tangible sense of advancement that can sometimes be lost in the broader scope of long-term projects. Each milestone achieved is a reminder that you're closer to your final goal, a psychological boost akin to a runner seeing the markers during a race. They slice through the potential overwhelm by focusing your energy on hitting the next achievable target, rather than getting tangled in the anxiety of the end game.

So, how do you set these milestones effectively? Start by mapping out your project and identifying its major phases.

Each phase should end with a deliverable that signifies its completion. These deliverables become your milestones. For example, if you're developing a new software feature, your milestones could be the completion of the design phase, the first successful code review, and the feature passing user acceptance testing. Each of these should be challenging enough to push you but achievable without causing burnout. It's like setting up a series of dominoes; you want to space them so they fall predictably, but with enough room to adjust as needed.

Now, celebrating these achievements is just as important as setting them. Every milestone reached deserves recognition. This isn't about throwing a party every time you complete a task, but about acknowledging the effort and the progress. Maybe it's taking an afternoon off, grabbing dinner at your favorite restaurant, or simply allowing yourself a guilt-free Netflix binge. These celebrations act as mental and emotional refresh points, giving you a well-deserved break and reinforcing the joy of accomplishment. They're your way of saying 'well done' to yourself, an important aspect of maintaining high spirits and motivation throughout the duration of a project.

Using milestones as evaluation points is another strategic move. Think of each milestone as a pit stop in a race. It's a chance to look back at the road traveled and forward to the road ahead. Ask yourself: What went well in this phase? What didn't? What have I learned that could make the next phase smoother? This reflection is crucial for continuous improvement and helps prevent the same hurdles from tripping you up repeatedly. It ensures that your project adapts and evolves, becoming more efficient and effective with each milestone.

This approach—setting, achieving, celebrating, and evaluating milestones—turns the daunting into the doable. It transforms projects into a series of steps rather than a giant leap and keeps your motivation burning bright from start to finish. So, as you look ahead to your next big project, remember the power of short-term milestones. They're not just markers on a path; they're celebrations of progress, reflections for growth, and most importantly, they're proof that no journey is too long when you take it one step at a time.

7.4 Reward Systems to Enhance Productivity

Picture your workday as a game where every task completion scores you points and those points can be cashed in for rewards. Sounds like a fun way to boost motivation, right? Well, that's essentially what building an effective reward system is all about. It's tailoring a set of incentives that not only propel you towards your goals but also make the journey enjoyable. Let's dive into setting up a system that sprinkles a little extra joy into your productivity process, tailored just for you.

The concept of reward systems is rooted in basic psychology—positive reinforcement. It's about linking a desired behavior, like completing a project phase, to a positive outcome, like a reward. This link makes the behavior more likely to be repeated. But here's the twist: the effectiveness of this system hinges on personalization. What motivates you? Is it a coffee break, a short walk, a weekend getaway, or perhaps just some good old-fashioned quiet time? Identifying what truly brings you joy is the first step in crafting a reward system that resonates with you.

Now, let's talk about the balance between immediate and delayed rewards. Immediate rewards (think a 15-minute break or a tasty snack after completing a task) are like quick sprints that keep your energy up throughout the day. They're your small wins, your instant gratifications that keep the engine running. On the other hand, delayed rewards (like a new book or a day off for hitting a major milestone) are more like the finish line of a marathon, something grand to look forward to, keeping you driven through the longer and often more arduous stretches of your projects.

Integrating these rewards into your daily routine requires a bit of strategy. It's about weaving your rewards so seamlessly into your workday that they propel productivity rather than distract from it. For instance, you might decide that after two hours of focused work, you'll treat yourself to your favorite coffee. Or, if you finish a challenging task ahead of schedule, you might take the rest of the afternoon off to relax or pursue a hobby. The key is to ensure these rewards do not derail your overall productivity but rather enhance it, keeping you motivated and engaged.

However, while rewards can be powerful motivators, there's a fine line between motivation and dependence. Relying too heavily on rewards can lead to a situation where your drive to work is entirely contingent on external incentives, not the intrinsic satisfaction of doing the work itself. To avoid this, it's crucial to gradually reduce the frequency of rewards while still maintaining their impact. Start by making the rewards less predictable. Instead of a reward for every task completed, switch to a variable schedule—maybe after three tasks, or at random, which can make the work itself more engaging and less about chasing rewards.

Reflection Section: Evaluate Your Reward Preferences

Take a moment to jot down five activities or items you find rewarding. Next to each, write down a task or milestone you could associate with that reward. This exercise helps you visualize and plan your reward system, making it a practical part of your productivity strategy.

By building a reward system that aligns with your personal preferences and integrating it thoughtfully into your daily routines, you transform your workday from a mere sequence of tasks into a more dynamic and enjoyable experience. This system not only boosts your productivity but also enhances your overall work satisfaction, making each day a little more rewarding.

As this chapter closes, we've equipped you with strategies not just for starting projects, but for powering through them with sustained momentum and strategically placed milestones, all peppered with rewarding moments that make the journey worthwhile. These tools are designed to keep you engaged, motivated, and on track, transforming project management from a daunting task to an enjoyable and rewarding process. With these strategies in hand, you're not just completing projects; you're mastering them.

Up next, we'll explore how to ensure that this isn't just a temporary boost but a sustainable part of your professional life. Stay tuned as we delve into creating lasting habits that keep your productivity soaring long after the initial excitement wanes. Let's keep this momentum going!

Key Takeaways

7.1 Overcoming Initiation Paralysis

- **Understanding the Challenge:** Initiation paralysis stems from fear of failure, overwhelm, and difficulty prioritizing.
- **Breaking Tasks into Smaller Steps:** Divide large tasks into manageable pieces to reduce mental load.
- **Using External Triggers:** Set specific times or use environmental cues to signal task initiation.
- **Developing a Pre-Task Routine:** Create a routine that prepares your brain for action, such as short meditation or physical warm-up.

7.2 Maintaining Momentum in Long-Term Projects

- **Revisiting Goals:** Regularly reflect on the project's goals and personal rewards to stay motivated.
- **Flexibility in Planning:** Adjust plans based on progress and setbacks, maintaining a steady pace towards completion.
- **Accountability Mechanisms:** Use regular check-ins with mentors or peers to enhance focus and commitment.

- **Reflection and Adjustment:** Periodically step back to review progress and make necessary adjustments to stay on track.

7.3 Setting and Achieving Short-Term Milestones

- **Importance of Milestones:** Break long-term projects into short-term goals to keep motivation fresh.
- **Effective Milestone Setting:** Identify major phases of the project and set deliverables for each phase.
- **Celebrating Achievements:** Acknowledge and reward progress to boost morale and motivation.
- **Evaluation Points:** Use milestones as opportunities to reflect on progress and improve strategies.

7.4 Reward Systems to Enhance Productivity

- **Concept of Reward Systems:** Link task completion to positive outcomes to enhance motivation.
- **Balancing Immediate and Delayed Rewards:** Use immediate rewards for quick gratification and delayed rewards for long-term motivation.
- **Integrating Rewards into Routine:** Plan rewards that enhance productivity rather than distract from it.

- **Avoiding Over-Reliance:** Ensure rewards support intrinsic motivation rather than replace it.

Chapter 8:

Advanced Networking and Social Skills

"You can make more friends in two months by becoming interested in other people than you can in two years by trying to get other people interested in you."

-Dale Carnegie

Ever walked into a networking event and felt like you were about to perform a tightrope act in front of a crowd without a safety net? That's often the experience for many of us with ADHD. Our minds are buzzing—a cocktail of thoughts, each vying for the spotlight—making the idea of engaging in small talk feel like a high-wire act. But what if I told you that mastering the art of small talk isn't just about keeping your balance but about setting the stage for deeper, more meaningful connections?

Let's turn that buzzing energy into a dynamic performance where every interaction is an opportunity to shine.

8.1 Mastering Small Talk with ADHD

Understanding the Role of Small Talk

Small talk is the appetizer of the networking world. It might not be the main course, but it sets the tone for the meal and, let's be honest, it can make or break the dining experience. In professional settings, these initial light conversations aren't just filler; they are crucial building blocks for relationships. They help us test the waters, gauge mutual interests, and establish a comfort zone with new acquaintances. Think of it as the warm-up act before the big show—it gets the audience (or in this case, your future connections) ready, relaxed, and engaged.

For professionals with ADHD, small talk can seem daunting. Our minds are often sprinting from one idea to another, making the slow pace of typical small talk feel jarring. But the beauty of small talk is that it's more about the connection than the content. It's not what you say about the weather that matters, but the rapport you build while discussing those cloudy skies.

Strategies for Initiating Small Talk

Initiating small talk is about finding common ground in a garden where the plants are topics like the weather, recent news, or the event itself. Start with open-ended questions that invite dialogue rather than simple yes or no answers. Questions like, "What brought you to this event?" or "What projects are you currently excited about?" open up the floor for a genuine exchange. They show your interest in the other person's thoughts and feelings, paving the way for a deeper conversation.

Using current events or mutual interests as conversation starters can also be a goldmine. Did a new piece of technology just hit the market? Is there a groundbreaking development in your industry? Bring it up! It not only shows that you're informed but also aligns you with the interests of your peers, creating a shared space for discussion. This tactic not just breaks the ice—it melts it.

Maintaining Engagement During Conversations

Now, keeping the ball rolling during small talk is an art form in itself. Active listening is your best tool here. This means really hearing what the other person is saying, not just planning what you'll say next. Reflect on their words, and follow up with questions or comments that show you're engaged. "That sounds like an exciting project! How did you get involved with that?" This kind of feedback turns a monologue into a dialogue, a ping-pong game of ideas that can lead to surprising and meaningful exchanges.

But what if the conversation starts to wane? Steering it can be as subtle as bringing up a related topic or sharing a brief, relevant anecdote. It keeps the energy up and prevents the dialogue from fizzling out. Think of it as gently nudging the conversation along a new path, one that might just lead to fascinating vistas.

Exiting Conversations Gracefully

All good things must come to an end, including conversations. Exiting gracefully is crucial because it leaves a lasting impression. Make your exit as memorable as your entrance with a polite closing statement that reflects the warmth of the interaction. Something like, "It's been great talking with you. I'd love to hear more about your work on [topic] sometime!" Not only does this signal the end of the conversation, but it also opens the door for future interactions.

And here's a little tip: exchanging contact information at this point can turn a transient chat into a lasting connection. Hand them your business card, or even better, send them a quick email on the spot. It's like saying, "I'm invested in this connection, and I value our interaction."

By mastering these elements of small talk, you transform what might seem like trivial chitchat into a powerful tool for building relationships. It's about taking those first awkward steps of conversation and turning them into a dance, where every move brings you closer to a rhythm of connections that can enhance your professional and personal life. So next time you find yourself at a networking event, remember: small talk isn't just talk; it's the small key that opens big doors.

8.2 Reading Social Cues in Professional Settings

Navigating the social waters of professional environments can sometimes feel like trying to read a book in a language you're only halfway fluent in. You catch the gist, but the subtleties? Those can slip right by. That's especially true for professionals with ADHD, where focusing on the spoken word is a task in itself, let alone decoding the silent language of body language, facial expressions, and tone of voice. Yet, these non-verbal cues are pivotal; they're the undercurrents that shape interactions and build relationships, making or breaking our connections with colleagues and clients.

Understanding what social cues are and their role in communication is akin to learning the rules of the road before you start driving. These cues, which range from a colleague's crossed arms during a meeting to the quick smile from a client after a presentation, are signals. They communicate feelings and attitudes that words might not fully convey. In professional settings, being attuned to these cues can mean the difference between a successful partnership and a missed opportunity. They help you gauge reactions, adapt your approach, and navigate interactions more effectively, ensuring you're not just speaking but truly communicating.

For professionals with ADHD, the rapid pace at which we process information can sometimes make it challenging to pick up on these subtler, slower-unfolding cues. But here's the good news: like any skill, reading social cues can be honed and improved with practice and awareness. Start by paying attention to the basics: body language, facial expressions, and tone of voice. Is your boss leaning in intently during your presentation, or are they looking out the window? Does your colleague's smile reach their eyes when they congratulate you, or does it flicker just above a grimace? These observations can tell you more about their true reactions than their words.

Interpreting these cues accurately often requires a bit of detective work. It's not just about noticing that someone is tapping their foot but figuring out why. Are they impatient, nervous, or just cold? This is where context comes into play. Foot tapping in a chilly, delayed morning meeting might just be an attempt to stay warm, while the same action during a heated budget discussion could signify impatience or anxiety. If you're unsure, don't hesitate to ask clarifying questions. A simple, "I noticed you seemed a bit uneasy when we discussed the budget, is there a particular concern you have?" can open the door to more direct communication and clear up misunderstandings before they escalate.

To sharpen these skills, consider setting up practice exercises or engaging in role-play scenarios, either alone or with a trusted friend or coach. For instance, you could watch a series of short videos or film scenes and try to note down all the non-verbal cues you observe. Discuss these with your practice partner and compare notes. What did you pick up on, and what did you miss? Why do you think that was? This kind of active practice not only improves your observational skills but also makes you more aware of how much can be communicated without words.

Turning these exercises into a regular practice can transform the way you interact with others. Over time, you'll find that reading and responding to social cues becomes more intuitive, allowing you to navigate professional settings with greater ease and confidence. You'll be better equipped to adjust your communication in real-time, tailoring your approach based on the feedback you're receiving non-verbally. This doesn't just make you a better communicator; it makes you a more empathetic colleague and a more effective professional, someone who doesn't just talk but truly connects.

8.3 Building and Maintaining Professional Relationships

Navigating the world of professional relationships can sometimes feel like trying to assemble a complex puzzle without the picture on the box for guidance. Sure, you've got the pieces—reliability, respect, mutual benefit—but figuring out how they fit together to create a sustainable, rewarding relationship can be a head-scratcher, especially when juggling the dynamic rhythms of ADHD. Yet, these relationships are foundational to career success, acting as the very scaffolding that supports your professional growth and opportunities.

Let's break it down, starting with the core elements. Reliability, the first piece of our puzzle, is about consistently delivering on your promises. It's showing up, both literally and figuratively, when you say you will. This builds a foundation of trust, and let's face it, trust is the currency in the economy of professional relationships. Next up, respect—this isn't just about being polite (though that's important too); it's about recognizing the value and contributions of others. It's listening to understand, not just to respond. And then there's mutual benefit. The best professional relationships aren't one-way streets; they're more like bustling highways, with ideas, support, and opportunities flowing freely in both directions.

Building trust is a marathon, not a sprint. It develops over time, through consistent interaction and shared experiences. One of the key strategies is, quite simply, to follow through. If you commit to a deadline, meet it. If you promise to check in, do it. This consistency is especially crucial for professionals with ADHD, as it helps to counter any misconceptions about our reliability due to our sometimes-erratic focus and energy levels. Transparency in communication is another trust-building tool. Be clear about what you can deliver and by when. If you hit a snag, communicate it—don't hide it. This honesty not only safeguards your integrity but also invites others to be equally open, creating a deeper, more authentic connection.

Now, even in the best-maintained relationships, challenges like misunderstandings or conflicts are inevitable. They're the weeds in our professional garden, popping up despite our best efforts. The key to managing these challenges, particularly with ADHD, where impulsivity or emotional reactivity can escalate conflicts, is to develop strong conflict-resolution skills. Active listening is a good start—it shows respect for the other person's perspective and helps clarify misunderstandings. When conflicts arise, approach them with a problem-solving mindset. Focus on the issue, not the person. Suggest solutions, and be open to compromise. This not only resolves the immediate issue but also strengthens the relationship by demonstrating your commitment to harmony and cooperation.

Maintaining these relationships over the long haul requires regular nurturing. Check in with your contacts, share updates or interesting finds, and celebrate their successes. This doesn't have to be a grand gesture—a quick note or a shared article can be enough to keep the connection alive and vibrant. Regular interactions keep you on each other's radar, which is crucial in today's fast-paced professional world where out of sight can quickly become out of mind. These check-ins also provide ongoing opportunities to reinforce your reliability, respect, and commitment to mutual benefit, which are the pillars upon which strong professional relationships are built.

Remember, each professional relationship you build is more than just a network connection; it's a bridge to new opportunities, a mirror reflecting your professional reputation, and a window into diverse perspectives and ideas. By investing in these relationships with intention and care, you not only enhance your career trajectory but also enrich your professional journey with meaningful interactions and mutual growth. So, take the time to nurture these connections. Your future self will thank you for it.

8.4 Strategies for Effective Online Networking

Navigating the digital landscape of networking can sometimes feel like trying to find your way in a bustling city where every street is bustling with potential connections and opportunities. Platforms like LinkedIn, Twitter, and various industry-specific forums are the skyscrapers in this metaphorical city, each offering a unique way to elevate your professional presence. Crafting a strong online profile isn't just about putting up a digital billboard of yourself; it's about constructing a dynamic, engaging narrative that draws others to you.

Creating a compelling professional profile is your first step. Think of your LinkedIn or any other professional profile as your personal homepage. This is where you tell your story, not just with a list of jobs and skills, but by weaving a narrative that highlights your achievements and the unique value you bring to your field. Use a professional photo where your confidence and approachability shine through. For the content, focus on accomplishments that are quantifiable and relevant. Managed a team? Speak to the successful outcomes. Improved sales or efficiency? Highlight the percentages. And don't forget to sprinkle your personality into it. A dash of personal interests or a touch of humor can make your profile memorable.

Engaging content is what will keep your network active and growing. Share articles, write posts, or create videos that reflect your professional insights or experiences. The key here is consistency and relevance. Become a resource in your field, someone who not only shares but also creates valuable content. This could be trend analysis, case studies, or even thought-provoking questions that spark discussions. Engaging doesn't mean you always have the final word; it means you're starting the conversation.

Now, the etiquette in these online interactions can be quite different from face-to-face. Timing, tone, and the type of media you use play pivotal roles in how your messages are perceived. Quick responses can be great, but they're not always necessary. Give yourself permission to take the time you need to craft thoughtful responses. Tone is trickier. Without the nuances of face-to-face interaction, written text can sometimes come across as cold or impersonal. Aim for a professional yet friendly tone, and when in doubt, lean towards clarity and kindness. As for multimedia, it's an excellent tool for making your communications stand out. A well-placed image, infographic, or video can transform a simple message into a standout piece of content. However, remember the key is relevance—make sure it enhances, not distracts from, your message.

Building connections virtually also requires strategy. Webinars, online workshops, and professional groups offer platforms not just for learning but for interacting. Participate actively. Ask questions, offer insights, and follow up with individuals who pique your interest. It's like mingling at a conference without having to leave your desk. These interactions, though virtual, can form the basis of solid professional relationships.

Maintaining these online relationships is crucial and often overlooked. Regular engagement is key. Comment on updates, congratulate achievements, and share content that adds value. Personal messages on birthdays or work anniversaries can add a personal touch that strengthens ties. And don't underestimate the power of virtual meetups. A quick video call can bridge the digital divide, creating a sense of real-time connection.

As you navigate this digital networking landscape, remember that each interaction is a brick in the building of your professional relationships. With a robust online presence, engaging content, and strategic interaction, you're not just building a network; you're cultivating a community that can grow with you throughout your career.

Reflecting on Online Networking

As we wrap up our exploration into the art of online networking, let's pause and reflect on the key aspects. We've traversed through creating impactful profiles, engaging effectively with content, understanding the nuances of online communication, and nurturing virtual connections. Each element plays a crucial role in transforming digital platforms from mere social spaces to powerful career-building tools.

Looking ahead, our journey will continue to unfold new strategies and insights that can enhance your professional life. In the next chapter, we'll delve into maintaining work-life balance—a critical component of sustainable success. By integrating the networking skills honed here with the holistic approaches we'll explore next, you're setting the stage for a thriving, balanced career that resonates with success on all levels. Stay connected, stay engaged, and let's continue to grow together.

Key Takeaways

8.1 Mastering Small Talk with ADHD

- **Importance of Small Talk**: Acts as a crucial icebreaker in professional settings, building rapport and setting the stage for deeper connections.
- **Initiating Small Talk**: Use open-ended questions about mutual interests or current events to engage in meaningful conversations.
- **Maintaining Engagement**: Practice active listening, reflect on others' words, and use follow-up questions to keep the conversation flowing.
- **Exiting Gracefully**: End conversations with polite closing statements and exchange contact information to build lasting connections.

8.2 Reading Social Cues in Professional Settings

- **Understanding Social Cues**: Non-verbal signals like body language, facial expressions, and tone of voice are crucial for effective communication.
- **Importance for ADHD Professionals**: Picking up on subtler cues can be challenging but is essential for successful interactions.

- **Improving Skills**: Practice observing and interpreting social cues through exercises, role-plays, and seeking feedback.
- **Real-Time Adjustments**: Responding to social cues intuitively can enhance communication and relationships in professional settings.

8.3 Building and Maintaining Professional Relationships

- **Core Elements**: Reliability, respect, and mutual benefit are foundational to strong professional relationships.
- **Building Trust**: Consistently deliver on promises, communicate transparently, and be open to feedback and compromise.
- **Handling Conflicts**: Use active listening and a problem-solving mindset to navigate misunderstandings and strengthen relationships.
- **Long-Term Nurturing**: Regularly check in, share updates, and celebrate successes to keep professional connections vibrant and mutually beneficial.

8.4 Strategies for Effective Online Networking

- **Creating a Compelling Profile**: Optimize your LinkedIn or professional profiles with a strong narrative, professional photo, and highlighted accomplishments.
- **Engaging Content**: Share relevant articles, write posts, and create videos to stay active and visible in your network.
- **Online Interaction Etiquette**: Craft thoughtful responses, maintain a professional tone, and use multimedia to enhance communications.
- **Building Virtual Connections**: Participate in webinars, online workshops, and professional groups to form solid relationships.
- **Maintaining Online Relationships**: Engage regularly, share valuable content, and use personal touches to strengthen ties.

Reflecting on Online Networking

- **Key Elements**: Effective profiles, engaging content, nuanced communication, and nurturing connections transform social media into career-building tools.
- **Looking Ahead**: Integrate networking skills with work-life balance strategies for a successful, balanced career.

Chapter 9:

Personal Success Stories

"I've missed more than 9,000 shots in my career. I've lost almost 300 games. 26 times, I've been trusted to take the game-winning shot and missed. I've failed over and over and over again in my life. And that is why I succeed."

- Michael Jordan

Imagine the vibrant, often chaotic world of arts, where creativity bursts like fireworks against the night sky. Now, picture artists, musicians, and writers who navigate this explosive creativity with a secret weapon—ADHD. Yes, that's right, the very traits often labeled as disruptive are the ones fueling some of the most innovative minds in the arts. Let's dive into the lives of these creative maestros, exploring how ADHD has not just shaped their artistic visions but propelled them into realms of unexpected brilliance.

9.1 Success in the Arts: Harnessing Creativity

Celebrating Creative Minds

Take, for instance Julian, a painter whose canvas is as wild and wide as her thoughts. Her ability to hyperfocus has allowed her to create detailed, immersive worlds that viewers can lose themselves in for hours. Then there's the musician whose mind skips from one melody to another, crafting symphonies that weave a tapestry of sound so intricate it could only come from a place of raw, unfiltered creativity. These artists leverage their ADHD-driven hyperfocus and divergent thinking to push boundaries and redefine norms, turning what many see as a disadvantage into their most potent tool.

But it's not just about the end product. The process, too, is imbued with a uniqueness that ADHD brings. Hyperfocus, often a hallmark of ADHD, allows these creative individuals to zone in on their work with an intensity that can lead to profound artistic expressions. Divergent thinking, another trait, enables them to connect disparate ideas, crafting pieces that speak in a thousand tongues, resonating with a myriad of audiences. This ability to see and connect patterns where others see randomness is what often sets their work apart, making it not just art but a statement.

Overcoming Artistic Challenges

Of course, the path isn't always strewn with rose petals. Many artists with ADHD grapple with disorganization and distractibility, the twins of chaos that can often disrupt the creative process. Yet, through personalized organizational systems and structured routines, they find their rhythm. One novelist, for instance, uses color-coded notes and meticulously organized files to map out her plots and characters, turning her whirlwind of ideas into bestselling narratives. Another artist sets strict studio hours, channeling what might otherwise be a scatter of artistic endeavors into periods of intense productivity.

These structured approaches do more than just tame the chaos; they provide a framework within which creativity can flourish unimpeded. By creating boundaries, these artists ensure that their energy is not wasted but instead directed towards creating something truly meaningful. It's about knowing when to let the mind roam free and when to rein it in, using ADHD's dynamic energy not as a hurdle but as a stepping stone to greater heights.

Impact of ADHD on Artistic Vision

The sensitivity to external stimuli, often overwhelming for many with ADHD, becomes a lens through which these artists view the world, noticing nuances that others might miss. This heightened perception feeds into their work, adding layers of depth and emotion that might be absent in more conventional pieces. For a sculptor, the texture of the clay speaks; for a photographer, the interplay of light and shadow tells a story. Each sensory experience is translated into art that speaks not just to the eyes or the ears but to the soul.

Such depth is evident in works that not only capture the beauty of the mundane but also the complexity of the human experience, often embodying the intense emotions that come with ADHD. The result is art that does more than entertain; it evokes, provokes, and invites reflection, leaving a lasting impact on its audience.

Strategies for Sustaining Creative Careers

Navigating a career in the arts with ADHD is much like riding the waves; it requires both flexibility and resilience. Artists find that balancing multiple projects, managing erratic schedules, and handling the highs and lows of creative work are all part of the package. Strategic planning, such as breaking down projects into phases or having clear, achievable milestones, helps in maintaining focus and momentum. Additionally, many artists find that regular collaboration with peers not only mitigates the isolation that can come with creative professions but also provides a support network that can be crucial during creative droughts or when dealing with rejection.

Moreover, embracing technology has allowed these professionals to streamline their creative processes and manage their careers more effectively. Digital tools for task management, social media for marketing and engagement, and online platforms for collaboration are all part of the modern artist's arsenal, helping them to not just survive but thrive in the fast-paced, ever-evolving world of art.

In the grand tapestry of the arts, those with ADHD are not just participants but pioneers, turning their vibrant inner worlds into expressions that challenge, delight, and inspire. Their stories are testaments to the power of embracing one's uniqueness, transforming potential stumbling blocks into stepping stones for success. Through their eyes, we see not just what is but what could be, in art and in life.

9.2 Achievements in the Sciences: Detail Orientation

Step into the world of laboratories and research facilities, where the air crackles with the energy of discovery and innovation. Here, scientists and researchers with ADHD are not just participants; they are often the trailblazers, turning their unique neurological wiring into a supercharged engine for scientific breakthroughs. Their ability to hyperfocus, often a hallmark of ADHD, allows them to delve deep into complex datasets and experiments, uncovering patterns and possibilities that might elude others. Their stories are not just about overcoming ADHD but about leveraging it to push the frontiers of science.

Detail-Oriented Scientific Minds

Consider the case of a researcher in neurology who, through the lens of her own experiences with ADHD, has pioneered a groundbreaking study on brain plasticity. Her ability to hyperfocus allowed her to spend countless hours analyzing micro-level changes in brain tissue, leading to insights that are reshaping our understanding of neural adaptation. Then there's the chemist whose rapid thought processes enable him to make intuitive leaps in synthetic chemistry, developing compounds at a pace that keeps his colleagues in awe. These scientists are meticulous, not despite their ADHD but because of it. Their focus and attention to detail, when channeled into their work, drive them to dig deeper and question further, often leading to novel findings that challenge conventional wisdom.

Navigating Scientific Challenges

Navigating the demanding world of science with ADHD involves more than just managing attention and focus. It requires turning potential obstacles into advantageous strategies. Take, for instance, a biologist studying complex ecosystems. The traditional approach might involve extensive, almost overwhelming amounts of data collection. However, by using her ability to hyperfocus, she develops a method to zero in on key indicators that can predict ecological changes, streamlining the research process significantly. Similarly, a physicist uses his propensity for rapid, divergent thinking to design experiments that test multiple hypotheses simultaneously, accelerating the research cycle and leading to faster iterations in his work.

Handling the sheer volume and complexity of data in scientific research can also be daunting. Yet, many scientists with ADHD develop unique systems to manage this challenge. They might use advanced data visualization tools that turn large datasets into comprehensible, visually engaging formats, helping them to see connections and trends that might not be obvious in raw numbers. Others set up meticulous, color-coded systems in their labs, where every test tube and petri dish has its place, turning potential chaos into a model of efficiency.

Role of ADHD in Innovative Research

The impulsivity and rapid thought processes associated with ADHD, often viewed as hurdles in everyday life, can become powerful catalysts for innovation in the scientific realm. These traits encourage bold thinking and risk-taking, essential for pioneering new research areas. For example, a researcher in renewable energy utilizes his impulsive curiosity to initiate a series of experimental projects on a new form of biofuel. While not all these ventures succeed, one leads to a breakthrough in energy efficiency, proving that sometimes, the best discoveries come from going off the beaten path.

Moreover, the ability to think differently, to make unconventional associations and leap beyond the obvious, often leads to the development of novel hypotheses that drive scientific innovation. This is seen in the work of an astrophysicist who posits a new theory on dark matter distribution that contradicts established models but is later validated by observational data. Such innovative thinking is not just about having intelligence or knowledge; it's about seeing the world through a different lens, a view often afforded by the unique cognitive style of those with ADHD.

Maintaining Focus and Productivity

Maintaining productivity in the demanding, detail-oriented world of science requires more than just passion and dedication; it requires practical strategies and tools. Many scientists with ADHD find that technology plays a crucial role in this aspect. They might use software that tracks experimental variables and results, ensuring that no detail is overlooked. Collaborative networks, both online and in-person, also provide vital support, offering new ideas and feedback that help refine research directions and maintain momentum.

Creating conducive work environments is another key strategy. This might mean structuring the laboratory space to minimize distractions, or setting specific times for deep-focus work, free from the interruptions of emails and meetings. Some scientists find that regular physical activity, such as jogging or yoga, helps them manage stress and boost concentration, keeping their minds sharp and ready for the challenges of their research.

In the realm of science, ADHD is not just a footnote; it is part of the main narrative for many researchers. It shapes how they view problems, how they tackle challenges, and how they make discoveries that can change the world. Their journeys are not about overcoming ADHD, but about embracing it, harnessing its unique qualities to fuel their scientific endeavors and achieve remarkable success.

9.3 Leadership in Business: Using ADHD to Innovate

Step into the dynamic world of business leadership, where thinking on your feet and making quick decisions often separates the good from the great. Now, imagine navigating this high-stakes environment with ADHD. Far from being a hindrance, many top entrepreneurs and business leaders have turned their ADHD into a superpower, driving innovation and strategic thinking that reshapes industries. These leaders, with their unique journeys and the challenges they've embraced, illustrate that ADHD can be a significant asset in the business world.

ADHD Leaders in Business

Picture a tech startup founder, whose brainstorms are as electric as the gadgets he designs, or a marketing guru whose campaigns capture the zeitgeist with uncanny precision. These are not just skilled professionals; they are maestros of innovation whose ADHD traits like rapid thought processing and risk-taking provide them with an edge. For instance, consider a CEO known for her disruptive business strategies, who credits her success to the hyperactive whirlwind of ideas that ADHD stirs in her mind. Each idea might not hit the mark, but her ability to generate and sift through them rapidly leads to pioneering strategies that keep her company ahead of the curve. These leaders often share stories of their early struggles with ADHD, how they felt out of place in traditional roles, and how embracing their natural inclinations towards innovation led them to the top. Their stories are not just inspiring; they are a playbook for turning perceived weaknesses into game-changing strengths.

Innovative Business Strategies

Innovation in business often requires a willingness to take risks and think outside the conventional box—traits that are second nature to many with ADHD. Take, for instance, a leader who transformed an ordinary logistics company into a tech-driven powerhouse. His secret? Leveraging his impulsivity to make quick decisions on tech investments, where slower-paced deliberations would have missed opportunities. Or consider a retail mogul who used her ADHD-driven urgency to revolutionize customer service in her stores, implementing a rapid response system that turned customer feedback into immediate action. These examples illustrate that the natural inclinations of those with ADHD to embrace risk and act swiftly can be powerful tools for business innovation, turning potential market downturns into opportunities for growth and development.

Building and Leading Teams

Leadership is not just about making decisions; it's about inspiring and managing a team to achieve shared goals. Here, the empathy and open communication often associated with ADHD come into play. These leaders excel in creating inclusive team environments that value open dialogue and feedback, where every team member feels heard and valued. They use their personal experiences with ADHD to foster a workplace culture that celebrates diverse thinking and learning styles, which in turn drives creativity and loyalty among their teams. For example, a tech CEO holds weekly brainstorming sessions where all employees, regardless of rank, are encouraged to pitch ideas. This not only taps into the collective creativity of the team but also demystifies the leadership process, making it more accessible and engaging.

Overcoming Business Hurdles

Navigating the daily grind of business management with ADHD involves a mix of clever strategy and personal insight. Effective delegation, time management, and decision-making are crucial skills that these leaders have honed to manage their ADHD in the workplace. They often share techniques like using visual aids and apps to manage their schedules and priorities or setting up clear, concise communication protocols to avoid misunderstandings and keep projects on track. Personal anecdotes from these leaders about their own trial-and-error journeys provide not just validation but also practical strategies that others can emulate. For instance, one entrepreneur uses a two-minute rule—if a task can be done in two minutes, he does it immediately, cutting down on procrastination and keeping his workflow smooth.

Navigating the complexities of business with ADHD isn't just about adapting; it's about thriving by turning unique challenges into avenues for innovation and leadership. These stories and strategies not only reshape our understanding of what it means to be a leader with ADHD but also inspire a new generation of professionals to embrace their differences and lead with confidence and creativity.

9.4 Military Precision: ADHD in Structured Environments

Imagine the regimented, disciplined world of the military—where orders are given and followed, where routines are not just encouraged but required, and where the stakes are incredibly high. Now, picture navigating this world with ADHD, where predictability meets the unpredictable nature of an ADHD mind. Surprisingly, many individuals find that the structured environment of the military is not just manageable but a place where they truly excel. The very traits of ADHD that might seem at odds with military discipline can, in fact, become substantial assets.

ADHD in the Military

Think about the intense focus that a crisis requires. Military personnel with ADHD often excel in these high-pressure situations, leveraging their ability to hyperfocus in moments of acute stress. This isn't just about coping; it's about thriving under pressure, where their hyperfocus aligns perfectly with the task at hand, whether it's navigating complex operations in the field or making split-second decisions that can save lives. The dynamic nature of military operations often complements the ADHD brain, which thrives on stimulation and activity. Rather than being overwhelmed, these individuals harness their natural intensity to perform tasks with a level of concentration and vigor that their peers might struggle to muster.

Adapting to Military Discipline

Now, adapting to the rigid structure of military life might sound like a challenge for someone with ADHD, known for impulsivity and a dislike for routine. However, many find that the clear rules and structured routines of the military create a framework that helps manage their symptoms. The predictability of routines reduces anxiety around the unknown, a common issue for those with ADHD, providing a sense of security and allowing them to focus their energy on the tasks at hand. Moreover, the impulsivity that might typically manifest as a challenge in civilian life transforms into a quick-reacting advantage in many military scenarios, where rapid response times are often crucial.

For instance, consider tactical operations where decisions need to be made quickly under stress; here, impulsivity can transition into a form of rapid decision-making. Military personnel with ADHD often develop strategies to channel their impulsivity into productive actions, using their quick thinking to respond to dynamic situations with agility and assertiveness. This ability to think and act swiftly is often enhanced by the adrenaline of critical operations, turning a potential ADHD drawback into a vital asset.

Leadership and Tactical Skills

Leaders with ADHD in the military are often innovative, thinking outside the conventional strategic box, which can lead to highly effective and unconventional tactics. Their ability to perform under pressure, combined with a natural inclination to rapidly assess and react to changing situations, makes them adept leaders in fluid combat scenarios. These leaders use their ADHD traits to foster a team environment that is flexible and responsive, encouraging initiative and quick thinking among their ranks.

Furthermore, their unique perspective can lead to enhanced problem-solving skills. ADHD fosters lateral thinking, a valuable asset in tactical planning where creative strategies can often outmaneuver more traditional approaches. These leaders often see connections and solutions that others might overlook, turning the fast-paced, ever-changing military environment into a canvas for strategic innovation.

Strategies for Success in Structured Settings

Success in such a demanding environment comes down to leveraging the right strategies. Many military personnel with ADHD find that embracing technological tools helps them maintain organization and manage responsibilities effectively. From digital calendars that keep track of schedules to reminder apps that alert them to deadlines and appointments, technology becomes an extension of their operational toolkit.

Another key strategy is the development of personal routines that segment their day-to-day tasks into manageable parts. These routines are tailored to align with their operational duties, allowing for flexibility within a structured framework. Moreover, they often employ physical exercise as a method to regulate energy levels and improve focus, integrating rigorous physical training into their daily schedule.

Innovation also plays a crucial role. Within the constraints of military rules, there is still room for personal refinement of processes and systems. Those with ADHD often excel in finding these small but impactful areas for improvement, enhancing efficiency and effectiveness in their roles. This continuous improvement mindset not only helps in personal career advancement but also contributes to the overall mission success.

By understanding and utilizing the strengths of their ADHD, military personnel not only thrive in this structured world but also reshape the very strategies and tactics that define military operations. Their journey is one of transformation, turning potential challenges into powerful advantages.

Reflection on Military Precision

As we wrap up this exploration into the intersection of ADHD and military precision, it's clear that the structured chaos of military life offers a unique backdrop against which the strengths of ADHD can shine. From hyperfocus and rapid decision-making to innovative leadership and strategic improvements, the traits of ADHD provide numerous advantages in this demanding field. The stories of these individuals underscore a broader narrative: with the right strategies and understanding, ADHD does not just fit into structured environments; it thrives, driving both personal and collective successes.

Key Takeaways

9.1 Success in the Arts: Harnessing Creativity

- **ADHD and Creativity**: ADHD traits like hyperfocus and divergent thinking fuel artistic innovation and profound expressions.
- **Celebrating Creative Minds**: Artists leverage ADHD to push boundaries and redefine norms, creating immersive, intricate works.
- **Overcoming Challenges**: Personalized organizational systems and structured routines help manage disorganization and distractibility.
- **Impact on Artistic Vision**: Heightened sensitivity to external stimuli enhances artistic depth and emotional resonance.
- **Sustaining Creative Careers**: Strategic planning, collaboration, and technology are essential for managing projects, schedules, and maintaining productivity in the arts.

9.2 Achievements in the Sciences: Detail Orientation

- **ADHD and Scientific Innovation**: ADHD traits like hyperfocus and rapid thought processes drive detailed and groundbreaking scientific research.
- **Detail-Oriented Minds**: Scientists leverage ADHD to uncover patterns and develop novel hypotheses, leading to significant discoveries.
- **Navigating Challenges**: ADHD scientists use advanced tools and systems to manage complex data and streamline research processes.
- **Innovative Research**: Impulsivity and bold thinking foster pioneering research and innovative solutions in scientific fields.
- **Maintaining Productivity**: Structured environments, technological tools, and collaborative networks help scientists with ADHD sustain focus and productivity.

9.3 Leadership in Business: Using ADHD to Innovate

- **ADHD in Business Leadership**: ADHD traits like rapid thought processing and risk-taking enhance strategic thinking and innovation.

- **Innovative Strategies**: Business leaders with ADHD leverage impulsivity for quick decision-making and transformative strategies.
- **Building and Leading Teams**: Empathy and open communication foster inclusive team environments, driving creativity and loyalty.
- **Overcoming Hurdles**: Effective delegation, time management, and decision-making strategies are crucial for managing ADHD in business.
- **Thriving with ADHD**: Business leaders turn ADHD challenges into strengths, leading with confidence and creativity.

9.4 Military Precision: ADHD in Structured Environments

- **ADHD in the Military**: ADHD traits like hyperfocus and rapid decision-making excel in high-pressure military situations.
- **Adapting to Discipline**: Clear rules and structured routines help manage ADHD symptoms in the military, providing predictability and reducing anxiety.

- **Leadership and Tactical Skills**: ADHD fosters innovative thinking and lateral problem-solving, enhancing tactical planning and leadership.
- **Success Strategies**: Embracing technology, developing personal routines, and continuous improvement are key for thriving in structured military environments.
- **Transforming Challenges**: Military personnel with ADHD turn potential challenges into powerful advantages, contributing to mission success and personal growth.

Reflection on Personal Success Stories

- **Harnessing ADHD Strengths**: Across various fields, individuals with ADHD turn their unique traits into powerful tools for innovation and success.
- **Strategic Management**: Personalized strategies and tools are essential for managing ADHD challenges and enhancing productivity.
- **Inspiration and Growth**: These stories highlight the potential of embracing ADHD, transforming obstacles into opportunities for remarkable achievements.

Chapter 10:

Tailored Strategies for Specific Careers

"Your work is going to fill a large part of your life, and the only way to be truly satisfied is to do what you believe is great work. The only way to do great work is to love what you do. If you haven't found it yet, keep looking. Don't settle. As with all matters of the heart, you'll know when you find it."

– Steve jobs

Ah, the creative life! Picture this: one moment you're sipping coffee, staring out the window, waiting for inspiration to strike. The next, you're a whirlwind of activity, ideas pouring out faster than you can capture them. This is the world of creative professions—unpredictable, thrilling, and devoid of that neat, predictable 9-to-5 structure. Whether you're a writer, artist, or freelancer, you know this rhythm well. It's like dancing to a tune that changes tempo every few beats. Exciting? Absolutely. Easy to manage? Not so much.

10.1 ADHD in Creative Professions: Managing Unstructured Time

Challenges of Unstructured Time

Let's face it, the freedom of unstructured time can be both a blessing and a curse. Without the external scaffolding of a typical office schedule, managing your time effectively becomes a bit like trying to catch smoke with your bare hands—frustrating and seemingly futile. You know the drill: one minute you're planning to start on that big project, and the next, you find yourself three hours deep into researching the migratory patterns of monarch butterflies. Interesting? Sure. Helpful for meeting your deadline? Not so much.

But here's the kicker: when you have ADHD, this swirl of unstructured time can feel even more daunting. Your brain's throttle is set to 'wander', making it an epic feat to steer it back to 'work mode' without those external cues to guide you. Yet, here you are, expected to navigate this nebulous time frame, producing masterpieces while also managing the mundane tasks of everyday life. It's like being asked to paint a mural with one hand while juggling fire with the other—possible, but oh boy, it's going to need some serious skill.

Implementing Structure

So, how do you tame this wild beast of creativity and unpredictability? The answer lies in creating a structure that mimics the external work environment you lack. It's about building a framework that supports your creative process while keeping those ADHD tendencies in check. Think of it as constructing a trellis for a vine; it can grow wildly, but with some guidance, it grows in the direction you want.

Start by setting fixed hours for your creative endeavors. These don't have to align with the traditional 9-to-5 but try to be consistent. Maybe you're a night owl, and your creative juices start flowing at midnight—great! Set your work hours from midnight to 3 AM. The key here is consistency. Your brain loves patterns, and by doing this, you're training it to kick into high gear at specific times.

Next, incorporate time-blocking techniques. Divide your workday into blocks dedicated to different tasks. Perhaps mornings are for brainstorming new ideas, afternoons for executing them, and evenings for administrative tasks like answering emails and scheduling posts. During each block, focus solely on the task at hand. This method not only helps manage your time effectively but also aligns beautifully with the ADHD brain's need for segmenting tasks to avoid overwhelm.

Tools for Self-Management

But let's amp up this strategy with some tech wizardry. There are fantastic tools and apps out there designed to keep your creative and professional life on track. Apps like Trello or Asana can help you manage projects by breaking them down into bite-sized tasks, complete with deadlines and reminders. Then there's Focus@Will, a service that provides music scientifically optimized to boost concentration and focus—perfect for when you need to drown out distractions and get into the zone.

For those spontaneous bursts of creativity that threaten to derail your well-planned schedule, keep a digital notepad or a simple app like Evernote handy to jot down ideas. This way, you capture your strokes of genius without letting them lead you off course. Then, schedule a time to explore these ideas further during your next brainstorming block. It's all about giving your creativity room to breathe without letting it run wild.

Balancing Creativity and Discipline

Balancing creativity and discipline are perhaps the trickiest part of navigating a creative career with ADHD. How do you maintain this delicate balance? By remembering that discipline is not the enemy of creativity but its enabler. Structure doesn't stifle creativity; rather, it channels it. It ensures that your brilliant ideas see the light of day rather than remaining eternally in the 'what if' phase.

Embrace routine check-ins with yourself, perhaps at the end of each week. Reflect on what you've accomplished, what's working, and what's not. Adjust your schedule and strategies as needed. Remember, flexibility is your friend. If a sudden flash of inspiration hits and you need to stray from your schedule, allow it—just steer back on course when you can.

Managing unstructured time in creative professions with ADHD is no walk in the park. But with the right strategies, tools, and a bit of self-compassion, you can create a work rhythm that not only sparks your creativity but also keeps it burning brightly and productively. After all, your creative mind is a wild horse—magnificent and free. With a gentle hand and a sturdy fence, you can let it run fast and far, in the directions that you choose.

10.2 ADHD in Technology Fields: Coping with Constant Change

Imagine standing in the middle of a tech expo, where every booth is buzzing with the latest innovations—virtual reality that can transport you to another world, gadgets that can automate your home, and software that promises to streamline your life. Now, if your brain is already a popcorn machine of thoughts, ideas, and impulses thanks to ADHD, this environment can feel both exhilarating and overwhelming. The tech field moves at the speed of light, and for professionals with ADHD, keeping up requires not just quick reflexes but a robust strategy.

Navigating this rapid change is like surfing; you need flexibility and balance. The tech industry's constant evolution can be stimulating, feeding the ADHD mind's hunger for new stimuli and quick wins. However, it also presents a significant challenge: staying current without getting swept away by the tide of never-ending updates.

Adaptability isn't just a nice-to-have in this game; it's the core skill that keeps you afloat.

To stay abreast of new technologies and industry changes without hitting the point of information overload, it's crucial to filter the noise. Not every trend or gadget is worth your bandwidth. Selective focus is your friend here. Identify trends that directly impact your work or spark your passion, and let go of the rest. This doesn't mean ignoring developments in the field; rather, it's about choosing your battles and your focus areas strategically. Curated learning resources can be invaluable in this regard. Subscribe to newsletters or follow thought leaders who align with your areas of interest. Platforms like Feedly or Pocket can help manage your information streams, ensuring you get to digest changes in digestible chunks.

Setting achievable learning goals is another key strategy. Break down your learning objectives into small, manageable milestones. If you're looking to master a new programming language or dive into the world of machine learning, set clear, incremental goals. Perhaps you could aim to complete a particular online course this month or build a small project using the new language in the next. These small victories not only keep you motivated but also make the immense world of tech feel a bit more manageable.

Now, let's talk about juggling multiple technology projects. In the digital realm, multitasking seems inevitable, but it's a notorious trap for the ADHD mind. To manage multiple projects without getting tangled in digital knots, advanced project management software is your best ally. Tools like Jira or Monday.com allow you to visualize project timelines, prioritize tasks, and get alerts on deadlines, all in one dashboard. But technology is only part of the solution. Prioritization frameworks are equally important. Learn to distinguish between urgent and important tasks—this can be the difference between spinning your wheels and actually moving forward. The Eisenhower Matrix, a simple yet effective tool, can help you sort tasks into categories and focus on what truly matters.

Delegation is another critical element. It can be tempting to hold onto every thread, especially when your mind is buzzing with ideas and possibilities. However, effective delegation can free you up to focus on tasks that match your unique strengths. Identify aspects of projects that can be handled by others, and articulate your expectations clearly.

This not only lightens your load but also empowers your team, creating a collaborative and efficient workspace.

Lastly, let's touch on stress management, an essential skill in an industry where burnout is all too common. High-change environments can amp up anxiety, particularly for the ADHD brain, which might already be on high alert. Mindfulness practices tailored to reduce anxiety can be a game-changer here. Techniques like guided meditation or breathing exercises can help recalibrate your stress response, making you more resilient in the face of tech tumult. Apps like Calm or Headspace offer guided sessions that can be squeezed into your coffee break, providing a quick mental reset.

Navigating the tech world with ADHD is not without its challenges, but with the right strategies, it can be incredibly rewarding. By harnessing your natural adaptability, focusing selectively, managing your projects smartly, and keeping stress at bay, you can not only survive but thrive in the ever-changing tech landscape. It's about riding the wave, not letting it ride you.

10.3 ADHD in Education: Strategies for Teachers

Imagine stepping into a classroom buzzing with energy, where each student's curiosity flits like a butterfly from one interest to another—this could easily describe a day in the life of a teacher with ADHD. Managing a classroom, planning lessons, and communicating effectively can feel like orchestrating a symphony in a hurricane. Yet, with the right strategies, it's not just possible to manage; you can truly excel and bring out the best in both yourself and your students.

Classroom Management with ADHD

First off, tackling the whirlwind of classroom activities demands a unique approach when you've got ADHD. Keeping track of multiple tasks and maintaining focus amidst the constant buzz of young minds can be daunting. The trick? Implement systems that reduce the cognitive load, allowing you to devote more energy to engaging with your students. Visual aids can be a game-changer here. Think about using color-coded systems for different subjects or activities. This not only helps you organize materials and tasks but also provides clear visual cues that can help keep your students on track.

Consider also the layout of your classroom. Arranging desks in a semi-circle or clusters can facilitate easier movement and interaction, allowing you to navigate the space efficiently and keeping those ADHD tendencies for hyperactivity harnessed positively. It's about creating a flow that matches your natural movement, reducing unnecessary stress and distraction.

Technology, too, can be a powerful ally. Digital tools that help track student attendance, submissions, and grading can streamline administrative tasks, freeing up more time for interactive teaching. Apps like Classroom Management Software not only keep you organized but also offer quick access to information, which is crucial when you need to make on-the-fly adjustments to your teaching plan.

Lesson Planning and Execution

Moving on to lesson planning and execution, the dynamic nature of ADHD might mean that sticking to a rigid plan feels counterintuitive. However, structure is crucial in education, and finding a balance is key. Start with a flexible lesson plan template that allows for spontaneity but covers all the essentials. Incorporate interactive elements like digital quizzes, group projects, and multimedia presentations that can keep you and your students engaged. These elements cater to different learning styles and keep the energy dynamic, which is perfect for maintaining your focus.

Incorporating movement and hands-on activities can also significantly enhance learning, especially in subjects that lend themselves to experiential learning, like science or art. Activities like role-playing historical events or conducting simple experiments not only make learning more engaging but also align with the energetic engagement style you might prefer due to ADHD.

Communication with Students and Parents

Effective communication is the cornerstone of educational success. Clear and open channels of communication with both students and parents are essential. With ADHD, maintaining clear communication can be challenging, especially when your mind is juggling a thousand thoughts. To manage this, set up regular intervals for updates and feedback. Digital newsletters or a class blog can be effective ways to keep parents informed about classroom activities and their child's progress. For in-person interactions, a bullet-point list of discussion topics can help keep meetings with parents focused and productive.

Moreover, establish a consistent protocol for students to ask questions or express concerns, whether it's a dedicated "office hour" or a question box where students can leave notes. This ensures that you address their needs without interrupting the flow of the class.

Self-Care and Burnout Prevention

Finally, self-care is crucial. Teaching is immensely rewarding, but it also requires a lot of energy, especially when you have ADHD. To prevent burnout, it's important to set boundaries between work and personal time. Use tools like digital calendars to block out time for breaks, exercise, and relaxation. Prioritize tasks and set realistic goals for each day or week. Remember, it's not about getting everything done at once but about maintaining a sustainable pace.

Utilize school resources, whether it's administrative support or professional development. Many schools offer resources for stress management and professional growth, which can provide you with strategies to manage your workload better and improve your teaching methods.

Navigating the educational field with ADHD presents unique challenges, but with these tailored strategies, you can create a thriving learning environment that leverages your strengths. By managing your classroom dynamically, planning engaging lessons, communicating effectively, and taking care of your well-being, you can transform potential obstacles into opportunities for growth and success.

10.4 ADHD in Healthcare: Managing High-Stress Environments

Step into the high-octane world of healthcare, where the pace is relentless and the stakes are sky-high. Here, professionals like you navigate the labyrinth of emergency rooms and intensive care units, where every second counts and the pressure can crush like a vise. But let's flip the script—what if your ADHD, with its fast-paced thinking and ability to hyper-focus under pressure, is not a hindrance but a superpower in this environment?

Coping with High-Stress Situations

Imagine the ER on a busy night—ambulances scream in, doctors dart from room to room, and you're at the center of this storm. Your ADHD brain, with its quick-fire neurons, is built for this. It thrives under pressure, turning chaos into a finely-tuned symphony of efficiency. But even superheroes need their strategies. First up, stress management—this is non-negotiable. Think of it as putting on your oxygen mask first. Techniques like tactical breathing, where you breathe in for four counts, hold for four, and exhale for four, can recalibrate your central nervous system, keeping panic at bay and allowing you to think clearly.

Next, visualization techniques can be a game-changer. Before your shift, take a moment to visualize it going smoothly—see yourself handling every crisis with calm and competence. This mental rehearsal primes your brain for performance, turning potential anxiety into a playbook of successful outcomes. And let's not forget about debriefs. After a high-intensity scenario, regroup with your team. Discuss what went well and what could be better next time. This isn't just about improving—it's about acknowledging the intense journey you've just navigated and giving your brain the closure it needs to reset and go again.

Time Management in Patient Care

Now, onto the ballet of time management in patient care. Here, efficiency is your best friend. Start with the ABCs—

Always Be Categorizing. Triage tasks not just by urgency but also by the type of focus they require. Use timers—set them for medication rounds, patient checks, or even to remind you to hydrate. These little pings of sound are like breadcrumbs, guiding you back to the path whenever your mind decides to go on a wander.

Scheduling strategies also take the spotlight. Structure your shifts around natural energy highs and lows. Tackle the most demanding tasks when your focus is laser-sharp, and save the less critical ones for when your mind starts to meander. And speaking of schedules, why not color-code them? Visual cues are like secret messages to your ADHD brain, cutting through the noise and helping you navigate your day.

Maintaining Focus During Long Shifts

Long shifts can be brutal—a marathon where the finish line keeps moving. So, how do you keep your focus sharp and your energy up? Strategic break-taking is key. Step away for five minutes every few hours. Stretch, breathe, or just close your eyes. These mini-breaks are like ctrl-alt-del for your brain, rebooting your system and boosting your focus.

Hydration and nutrition are your fuel. Keep water on hand always, and choose snacks that release energy slowly—think nuts, fruits, or yogurt. Avoid the sugar trap; it's a quick high but an even quicker crash. And for those long nights, consider noise-canceling headphones. Whether you're charting or preparing medications, they can help mute the chaos around you, allowing you to focus on the task at hand.

Emotional Regulation and Resilience Building

Finally, let's talk about safeguarding your emotional health. Healthcare is not just physically demanding; it's an emotional rollercoaster. Building resilience is about creating a buffer against this strain. Start with peer support groups. These are your fellow warriors, the only ones who truly understand the trenches you navigate daily. Share your experiences, vent, listen, and support each other. Professional counseling can also provide a safe space to unpack the emotional baggage that comes with the job.

And don't underestimate the power of stress-relief practices. Whether it's yoga, meditation, or just a walk after your shift, find what helps you decompress and make it a non-negotiable part of your routine. These practices are not just about relaxation; they're about building a fortress around your mental health, ensuring you're as strong emotionally as you are professionally.

Navigating the high-stress world of healthcare with ADHD might seem daunting, but remember, your brain is uniquely equipped for this challenge. With the right strategies, you can not only manage but excel, turning what might seem like obstacles into stepping stones for success. As you continue to harness these skills, you pave the way not just for a thriving career but for a fulfilling life, both in and out of scrubs.

Wrapping Up: From Chaos to Control

As we close this chapter, remember that your journey in healthcare is about transforming chaos into control. The strategies discussed here are your tools to not just survive but thrive in the bustling corridors of hospitals and clinics. Each day presents new challenges, but with your unique abilities and these tailored techniques, you're more than ready to meet them. Stay tuned for more insights in the next chapter, where we'll explore even more ways to leverage your ADHD in professional settings. Here's to turning every challenge into a victory.

Key Takeaways

10.1 ADHD in Creative Professions: Managing Unstructured Time

- **Challenges of Unstructured Time**: The freedom of unstructured time can be both a blessing and a curse, making it difficult to manage deadlines and productivity.
- **Implementing Structure**: Create a consistent schedule tailored to your creative rhythm and use time-blocking techniques to focus on different tasks throughout the day.
- **Tools for Self-Management**: Utilize apps like Trello, Asana, and Evernote for project management and idea capture. Use Focus@Will for concentration-enhancing music.
- **Balancing Creativity and Discipline**: Embrace discipline as a way to channel creativity, use routine check-ins for self-reflection, and remain flexible to accommodate sudden bursts of inspiration.

10.2 ADHD in Technology Fields: Coping with Constant Change

- **Navigating Rapid Change**: The fast-paced tech industry requires selective focus and adaptability to manage constant innovations without feeling overwhelmed.
- **Staying Current**: Filter information by focusing on relevant trends and set achievable learning goals using curated resources and incremental milestones.
- **Managing Multiple Projects**: Use advanced project management tools like Jira or Monday.com, and employ prioritization frameworks like the Eisenhower Matrix to distinguish urgent tasks.
- **Delegation and Stress Management**: Delegate tasks effectively, use mindfulness practices to manage stress, and employ strategies like guided meditation for quick mental resets.

10.3 ADHD in Education: Strategies for Teachers

- **Classroom Management**: Implement visual aids, organize classroom layouts efficiently, and use technology to streamline administrative tasks.

- **Lesson Planning and Execution**: Use flexible lesson plans with interactive elements, incorporate movement and hands-on activities, and cater to different learning styles.
- **Communication with Students and Parents**: Maintain clear communication through regular updates, use digital newsletters, and establish protocols for student interactions.
- **Self-Care and Burnout Prevention**: Set boundaries between work and personal time, utilize school resources, and engage in stress management practices to prevent burnout.

10.4 ADHD in Healthcare: Managing High-Stress Environments

- **Coping with High-Stress Situations**: Use stress management techniques like tactical breathing and visualization to stay calm and focused in high-pressure scenarios.
- **Time Management in Patient Care**: Categorize tasks by urgency, use timers and color-coded schedules, and structure shifts around natural energy highs and lows.

- **Maintaining Focus During Long Shifts**: Take strategic breaks, stay hydrated, choose healthy snacks, and use noise-canceling headphones to reduce distractions.
- **Emotional Regulation and Resilience Building**: Engage in peer support groups, professional counseling, and stress-relief practices like yoga and meditation to maintain emotional health.

Reflection on Navigating Professions with ADHD

- **Harnessing ADHD Strengths**: Across various fields, individuals with ADHD can turn their unique traits into powerful tools for innovation and success.
- **Strategic Management**: Implementing personalized strategies and tools is essential for managing ADHD challenges and enhancing productivity.
- **Inspiration and Growth**: These stories highlight the potential of embracing ADHD, transforming obstacles into opportunities for remarkable achievements.

Chapter 11:

Integrating Technology and Tools

"Technology is the best thing that ever happened to humans."

- Elon Musk

Picture this: you're at your desk, the clock's ticking, and your computer screen looks like a digital version of Times Square on New Year's Eve. Tabs open, reminders pop up, and you're trying to focus like a cat watching a laser pointer dance wildly on the wall. Welcome to the ADHD experience in our hyper-connected world! Now, wouldn't it be great if there were magic wands—or, let's be real, apps—that could streamline this chaos into something that not only makes sense but actually boosts your productivity? Good news: such tools aren't just figments of digital fantasy. They exist, and they're here to make your life a whole lot easier.

11.1 Apps for Time Management and Focus

Overview of Time Management Apps

Let's dive into the digital toolbox and explore some of the coolest apps designed to keep you on track. Time management apps are like having a personal assistant who's always on the ball, even when your mind wants to play ping-pong with your tasks. These handy helpers come equipped with features like task timers, which can be a godsend for pacing your work sessions. Reminders? Check. They'll nudge you gently (or not so gently) about deadlines and meetings, so you're not caught off guard. And scheduling functionalities? They turn the art of planning from a dreaded chore into a neatly organized dance of alerts and blocks of time that even your scattered brain can appreciate.

Now, you might think, "But I've tried apps before, and they just add to the clutter!" That's where customization swoops in to save the day. Most time management apps today offer a degree of personalization that can make them feel like they were built just for you. You can set more frequent reminders or adjust focus intervals to match the ebb and flow of your attention span. It's like having a tailor for your digital needs, ensuring everything fits just right.

Focus-Enhancing Apps

Moving on to focus-enhancing apps, these are your allies in the battle against the sirens of distraction that call your name all day. Whether it's social media notifications or the enticing rabbit hole of internet research, these apps can help shield you from distractions. Some block access to time-sucking websites during work hours, while others provide ambient sounds to drown out disruptive noise. Ever tried working to the soothing sounds of rain or a bustling café? It's quite an experience and can dramatically increase your focus.

And for a touch of fun, there are apps that use gamified focus techniques. Imagine planting a virtual tree that grows as you focus on your tasks. If you wander off to check the latest viral video, your tree withers. It's a simple yet powerful visual incentive to keep your eyes on the prize (or, in this case, on the tree).

Customization for ADHD Needs

But here's where it gets really interesting. Customization is key for making these apps work for you, not against you. You can often adjust settings to create a user experience that caters specifically to your ADHD brain. Need to break down your workday into hyper-focused sprints? There's an app setting for that. Prefer continuous, gentle reminders throughout the day to keep you on track? Yep, that's an option too.

Case Studies of Successful Usage

Let's talk real life. Consider Alex, a graphic designer with ADHD who swears by a popular time management app. Before using the app, Alex struggled with missed deadlines and constant stress from juggling multiple projects. Now, with customized reminders and the ability to visually map out his day, he's not only meeting deadlines but also finding time for breaks, which has significantly improved his overall well-being and creativity.

Or take Priya, a software developer who uses a focus-enhancing app that blocks distracting sites and sounds during her coding marathons. She customizes the app's focus sessions to match her peak productivity times, resulting in a noticeable uptick in her output and a decrease in her usual work-related frustrations.

These stories underscore a crucial point: with the right tools and a bit of tweaking, managing your time and maintaining focus isn't just a possibility—it's a game changer. By integrating these apps into your daily routine, you're setting up a framework that supports your unique working style, turning potential ADHD pitfalls into stepping stones for success. And isn't that what we all strive for—finding our rhythm in this fast-paced digital symphony?

11.2 Tools for Organizational Efficiency

Let's talk about the digital sidekicks that can make your life a heck of a lot smoother. I'm referring to those digital organizers and planners that, unlike their paper ancestors, can do much more than just keep dates. Imagine never having to erase a cancelled appointment again or seamlessly shifting a whole week of meetings with a few clicks. These digital tools are not just about keeping dates; they're about syncing your entire life across all your devices. This means you could add an appointment on your phone while in line for coffee and have it pop up later on your laptop during planning. It's like having a personal assistant who's always in sync with you, minus the coffee runs.

The real kicker? These tools integrate beautifully with other apps. Say you schedule a meeting in your digital planner; it can automatically pull in emails from those attendees, show you the last document you collaborated on, and even remind you to follow up on tasks discussed last time. It's about connectivity and making sure all the dots in your professional (and, why not, personal) life are connected. This isn't just convenience; it's about creating a seamless flow of information that keeps you ahead of the game without you needing to micromanage every part of the process.

Moving on, let's dive into the world of project management tools. If you've ever felt like you're juggling a dozen balls with only two hands, these are for you. These tools are designed to give you a clear visual overview of all your projects. We're talking color-coded tasks, progress bars, and dashboards that show you at a glance what's under control and what needs your attention. And for professionals with ADHD, this visual aspect is a game-changer. It transforms abstract concepts like time and progress into something you can see and almost touch, making it much easier to manage.

But it's not just about pretty graphs and charts. These tools come with features like task dependencies, which help you understand how one task affects another, and automated alerts that remind you not to start the budget report before the data analysis is complete. It's like having a coach who reminds you of the play before you run it, ensuring you're always on the right track and never dropping the ball.

Now, let's talk about automating those pesky routine tasks that eat up your precious time. I mean, who wants to spend hours sorting emails or scheduling appointments when you could be brainstorming the next big project or, let's be honest, catching up on your favorite series? Automation tools can handle these tasks with a level of efficiency that frees up your cognitive load for more important matters. Email sorting tools use algorithms to categorize your inbox into priorities, appointments, and even spam, making sure you only focus on what's truly important.

And when it comes to scheduling, these tools are like having a diplomatic negotiator in your corner. They find the perfect time slot that works for everyone involved, send out invites, and even reschedule if someone can't make it. It's about removing the friction from administrative tasks and streamlining processes that otherwise chip away at your focus and energy.

Recommendations and Resources

To wrap this up, let's make sure you have everything you need to get started. Here are some tools I personally recommend: For digital organizing, check out Asana for its user-friendly interface and powerful integration capabilities. If project management sounds like your next best friend, Trello offers an intuitive visual card-based system that makes managing projects almost fun. And for automation? Zapier can connect the apps you use daily, automating workflows and ensuring your digital life runs smoothly without constant oversight.

Remember, the right tools can transform the way you work and live, especially when dealing with ADHD. They can bring order to chaos, focus to distraction, and calm to the constant storm of tasks and deadlines. So go ahead, arm yourself with these digital powerhouses, and turn your day-to-day challenges into well-orchestrated symphonies of productivity.

11.3 Gadgets That Improve Workplace Productivity

Let's talk about the unsung heroes of the modern workspace: gadgets. Not just any gadgets, but those nifty little devices that seem to have a secret pact with your ADHD brain, helping you manage time and maintain focus. If you've ever felt like your workspace was a second home, these gadgets are your friendly neighbors, making sure you're comfortable and productive.

Wearable Technology

Starting with wearable technology, think of smartwatches and fitness trackers as your personal coaches. They're not just about counting steps or monitoring your heart rate; they're about keeping you on track with gentle reminders. Ever found yourself so engrossed in a task that you missed a meeting or forgot to grab lunch? Your smartwatch won't let that happen. Set reminders for meetings, use apps to block out focus times, and even get nudged when it's time to stand up and stretch. It's like having a personal assistant on your wrist—one that's invested in keeping your day running smoothly and healthily. Plus, monitoring your health routines can directly impact your productivity. Better sleep and more active breaks can enhance your focus, and these gadgets provide the data you need to make informed adjustments to your lifestyle. It's all about creating a healthy rhythm that keeps your mind sharp and ready to tackle any challenge.

Desktop Gadgets

Moving to your actual work station, let's deck out your desk with some ADHD-friendly gadgets. Standing desk converters, for instance, are a game-changer. If you're someone who gets restless easily, switching between sitting and standing can keep your body engaged and your mind active. Then, there are desk organizers with built-in charging ports—no more cluttered cables or dying devices mid-Zoom call. And let's not forget about focus lights. These aren't your average desk lamps; they're designed to enhance concentration with temperatures and brightness that mimic natural daylight, keeping your internal clock in check and reducing eye strain.

Each of these gadgets serves a dual purpose: they organize your physical space and streamlines your workflow. Clutter can be a major distraction, and by keeping your workspace tidy and functional, you're setting the stage for focused, productive work sessions. Think of your desk as the cockpit of a plane; every instrument and control is exactly where you need it, allowing you to navigate your workday with precision and ease.

Customizable Lighting and Sound Devices

Now, let's brighten things up a bit—literally. Adjustable lighting systems can transform your workspace from a dreary cave to a vibrant studio with the slide of a dimmer or the tap on app. Different tasks require different lighting. For instance, warm, dim lights might be great for winding down with some reading, but when you're crunching numbers or drafting emails, you'd want clear, bright light that keeps your mind alert. And when the outside world gets too noisy, sound-masking devices can be your sanctuary. These devices use white noise or natural sounds to drown out distracting background chatter, making it easier to focus on the task at hand. Whether it's the hum of a busy café or the soothing sound of rain, creating an auditory environment that enhances your concentration can significantly boost your productivity.

Evaluating Gadgets for Personal Use

Choosing the right gadgets can feel like navigating a tech expo. Start by assessing your daily needs and challenges. Do you lose track of time easily? Consider a smartwatch. Struggle with sitting still during long work sessions? A standing desk converter might be your new best friend. Think about your work habits, your sensory preferences, and even the physical layout of your workspace. Budget and space are also crucial considerations. Not everyone can transform their home office into a mini-NASA control room, and that's okay. Start small—maybe with a multifunctional desk organizer or a simple focus light—and gradually build a collection of gadgets that truly make a difference in your day-to-day productivity.

Incorporating these gadgets into your workspace isn't just about staying organized or on schedule; it's about creating an environment that resonates with your unique way of functioning. It's turning your workspace into a zone where your ADHD doesn't feel like a barrier but rather a different way of engaging with the world—one that is vibrant, dynamic, and beautifully efficient.

11.4 Using Social Media for Professional Growth

In the buzzing digital bazaar that is social media, the right strategy can transform your professional presence from a whisper in the wind to a commanding voice at the conference table. For professionals with ADHD, the dynamic nature of social media platforms like LinkedIn, Twitter, and YouTube is a double-edged sword. It's a space ripe with opportunities to showcase our unique perspectives and creative flares, but without a game plan, we can easily get lost in the noise or, worse, succumb to the vortex of endless scrolling.

Strategic Use of Social Media

Let's kick things off with LinkedIn, the coliseum of professional networking. Optimizing your LinkedIn profile is like dressing up for the job you want. Start with a professional photo that says, 'I mean business'. Your headline? Make it snappy and specific. Think of it as your personal tagline—what are you about? Dive into the summary section with gusto. This is your elevator pitch: who are you, what have you achieved, and what are you aiming for? Be bold, be bright, and be memorable.

But don't just polish your profile and call it a day. Engage actively. Comment on posts in your field, share interesting articles, and maybe drop a thought-provoking post or two yourself each week. Engagement shows you're not just a resume; you're a voice in your industry. And here's a tip: set a timer for your LinkedIn activities. It's easy to get sucked in, but remember, the goal is strategic engagement, not digital wandering.

Content Creation and ADHD

Now, flipping over to content creation—this is where your ADHD brain can really shine. Platforms like blogs, Twitter, or YouTube are perfect canvases for your rapid-fire thoughts and boundless creativity. Start a blog where you dive deep into topics, you're passionate about. Or perhaps launch a YouTube channel where your dynamic personality can bring those topics to life. Twitter, with its fast-paced dialogue, can amplify your voice in industry conversations.

The secret sauce? Authenticity. Let your unique voice and perspective lead the way. People cling to content that resonates on a personal level and that tells a story. Your ADHD gives you a unique lens on the world—use it. Tell stories about your professional challenges and victories, share tips that have worked for you, or give insights into the latest industry trends. Remember, consistency is key. Regular posts keep your audience engaged and help establish your presence as a thought leader in your space.

Managing Online Presence

But as the digital landscape thickens, managing your time on these platforms becomes crucial. It's easy to fall down the rabbit hole of social media, losing hours meant for other tasks. Use tools like Hootsuite or Buffer to schedule your posts ahead of time. This not only saves you time but also helps maintain a consistent presence online without the need to be constantly logged in.

Set boundaries for your social media activities. Maybe decide that 20 minutes in the morning and another 20 in the late afternoon are all you'll spend on social media. Use a timer to keep yourself honest. And be strategic about when you post—aligning your schedule with when your audience is most active enhances engagement without necessitating more screen time.

Leveraging Social Media for Learning and Development

Beyond networking and personal branding, social media is a treasure trove of learning opportunities. Join groups and forums on LinkedIn that are relevant to your industry. These can be goldmines of information and new trends, providing a platform for learning and discussion. Participate in webinars; these are often advertised on LinkedIn and can be a great way to enhance your skills and knowledge.

Following industry leaders and influencers on platforms like Twitter can also provide daily nuggets of wisdom and keep you updated on industry shifts. Engage with their content, ask questions, and participate in discussions. Every interaction is a learning opportunity and a chance to deepen your understanding of your field.

In essence, when wielded wisely, social media is more than a tool for networking and personal branding—it's a continuous loop of opportunity for growth, learning, and professional development. As you harness these digital platforms, remember that they are instruments in your larger career orchestra. Play them well, and the symphony of your professional life will resonate impressively across the digital and real-world stages.

Wrapping Up: From Digital Footprints to Career Pathways

As we wrap up this exploration of leveraging social media for professional growth, remember that each post, tweet, or video is a brick in the edifice of your career. When used strategically, social media not only enhances your visibility but also expands your learning horizons and connects you to a global community. Keep your digital engagements rich with content, purposeful in interaction, and balanced in time investment. Onward now to the next chapter, where we'll explore advanced strategies for turning these digital engagements into tangible career advancements. Here's to building a vibrant, impactful online presence that mirrors your professional aspirations and achievements!

Key Takeaways

11.1 Apps for Time Management and Focus

- **Overview of Time Management Apps**: Time management apps act like personal assistants, offering task timers, reminders, and scheduling functionalities to keep you on track.
- **Focus-Enhancing Apps**: These apps help block distractions and provide ambient sounds to enhance focus, sometimes gamifying the focus process to keep you engaged.
- **Customization for ADHD Needs**: Apps can be customized to fit your ADHD-specific requirements, such as frequent reminders or hyper-focused work sessions.
- **Case Studies of Successful Usage**: Examples include Alex, a graphic designer, and Priya, a software developer, who both found significant improvements in productivity and stress reduction through the use of customized apps.

11.2 Tools for Organizational Efficiency

- **Digital Organizers and Planners**: These tools sync across devices, integrate with other apps, and help streamline your professional life by managing dates, tasks, and reminders.
- **Project Management Tools**: Tools like Trello and Asana provide visual overviews of projects with color-coded tasks and progress bars, making it easier to manage multiple projects.
- **Automation of Routine Tasks**: Automation tools can sort emails, schedule appointments, and handle other routine tasks, freeing up time for more important activities.
- **Recommendations and Resources**: Recommended tools include Asana for digital organizing, Trello for project management, and Zapier for automation.

11.3 Gadgets That Improve Workplace Productivity

- **Wearable Technology**: Smartwatches and fitness trackers can help keep you on track with reminders and monitor health routines to boost productivity.

- **Desktop Gadgets**: Gadgets like standing desk converters, desk organizers with charging ports, and focus lights help create a functional and organized workspace.
- **Customizable Lighting and Sound Devices**: Adjustable lighting systems and sound-masking devices enhance concentration and reduce distractions.
- **Evaluating Gadgets for Personal Use**: Choose gadgets based on your daily needs and challenges, considering budget and workspace limitations.

11.4 Using Social Media for Professional Growth

- **Strategic Use of Social Media**: Optimize your LinkedIn profile with a professional photo and detailed summary. Engage actively by commenting on posts and sharing interesting articles.
- **Content Creation and ADHD**: Use blogs, Twitter, or YouTube to share your unique perspectives and stories, maintaining authenticity and consistency.
- **Managing Online Presence**: Use tools like Hootsuite or Buffer to schedule posts and set boundaries to avoid spending excessive time on social media.

- **Leveraging Social Media for Learning and Development**: Join relevant groups and forums, participate in webinars, and follow industry leaders for continuous learning and professional development.

Reflection on Leveraging Technology and Tools for ADHD

- **Harnessing ADHD Strengths**: Technology and tools can help turn ADHD challenges into strengths by providing structure, enhancing focus, and streamlining tasks.
- **Strategic Management**: Customization and strategic use of these tools are key to maximizing productivity and maintaining balance.
- **Inspiration and Growth**: Real-life examples and practical strategies highlight the potential for significant improvement in professional and personal life when leveraging these tools effectively.

Chapter 12:

Long-Term Career Planning with ADHD

"Someone is sitting in the shade today because someone planted a tree a long time ago."
- Warren Buffet

Imagine you're setting out to build a magnificent castle, not from stones or mortar but from your career achievements and experiences. Just like a master builder, you need a plan, tools, and flexibility to adapt as your structure takes shape, especially when the winds of ADHD blow unpredictably. This chapter is about laying that foundation, crafting sturdy walls, and ensuring that your career castle not only stands tall but also reflects your unique architectural flair.

12.1 Setting Career Goals with ADHD

Understanding Achievable Goals

Setting goals when you have ADHD can sometimes feel like trying to pin the tail on a very active, very invisible donkey. You know there's a target, but hitting it seems like a game of chance. However, when you break down the process and use the right strategies, goal-setting transforms from a game of luck into a science of success. One effective framework is the SMART criteria, which stands for Specific, Measurable, Achievable, Relevant, and Time-bound goals.

Here's the kicker: goals for individuals with ADHD need to be even SMARTER. Yes, that's right! They need to be exciting enough to capture your fleeting attention. For instance, rather than setting a goal like "increase sales," a more ADHD-friendly goal might be "introduce one innovative sales strategy per month that taps into emerging market trends." This type of goal is not only specific and measurable but also interesting enough to keep you engaged.

Long-Term vs. Short-Term Goals

The relationship between long-term and short-term goals can be likened to a treasure map, where short-term goals mark the path to the X that marks your treasure, your long-term aspirations. For someone with ADHD, the thrill often lies in the hunt and the series of discoveries along the way. This means that while the long-term goal provides direction, the short-term goals need to be particularly engaging and rewarding to maintain motivation.

The structure here is crucial. Short-term goals should act as stepping stones that build your confidence and skills progressively, leading towards your larger ambition. For example, if your long-term goal is to become a department head, a short-term goal might be to lead a small project team successfully. This setup helps in managing ADHD traits like fluctuating motivation and interest levels, ensuring that you remain engaged and on track.

Incorporating Flexibility

Flexibility is your secret weapon. It's about building a career plan robust enough to stand firm against the winds of change yet flexible enough to sway when the unexpected storms of ADHD hit. This could mean setting adjustable timelines or having contingency plans ready. For instance, if you're working on a project that's suddenly hit by a wave of unexpected challenges (hello, ADHD!), having a built-in buffer period for project completion can be a lifesaver.

Flexibility also applies to how you perceive and adjust your goals. With ADHD, interests and passions can shift, and what was motivating a year ago might not spark the same enthusiasm now. Allow yourself the creative freedom to realign your goals without feeling like you're starting over. Think of it as recalibrating your GPS when you hit a roadblock or discover a more scenic route.

Goal-Setting Workshops and Tools

Since goal-setting isn't a solo journey, consider engaging in workshops or using online courses designed to keep you accountable and provide structured guidance. Look for resources that are ADHD-friendly, which often means they are interactive, engaging, and broken down into digestible segments. Tools like Trello or Asana can help you track your goals visually, making the process less daunting and more accessible.

An interactive element here could be setting up a goal-setting dashboard using one of these tools. This dashboard can serve as a visual reminder of your goals, progress, and the flexible paths you can take to achieve them. It's both a tool and a motivator, keeping you engaged and organized—a dual necessity for managing ADHD in the long haul of career planning.

In wrapping up this section, remember that setting goals with ADHD isn't about chaining yourself to a rigid list of to-dos. It's about creating a lively, flexible map that invites you to explore and expand, turning what might seem like wild, untamed paths into routes towards success. Whether it's through SMART goals, balancing the scales between short-term wins and long-term visions, or using digital tools to keep track of your progress, the strategy remains the same: tailor the process to fit your unique way of interacting with the world, turning potential obstacles into stepping stones for achievement.

12.2 Long-Term Skill Development Strategies

Navigating your career with ADHD can sometimes feel like you're trying to play an intense game of dodgeball. Just when you think you've got a handle on things, whoosh! A new challenge or opportunity flies by, demanding a quick pivot or a strategic leap. It's exhilarating, unpredictable, and requires a keen understanding of both your strengths and the skills you need to develop. Identifying these key skills isn't just about listing what you're good at or what interests you. It's about deeply understanding how your unique ADHD traits, like rapid problem-solving and resilience, intersect with the skills demanded by your chosen field.

Let's break it down: imagine you're in a profession that values quick decision-making and innovative solutions—areas where your ADHD brain can really shine. Here, your natural ability to think outside the box is a significant asset. But what about the skills that might not come as naturally? Maybe detailed record-keeping makes you want to run for the hills, or perhaps maintaining focus during repetitive tasks feels like a Herculean effort. This is where strategic skill development comes into play. By pinpointing where your natural talents can be augmented with learned skills, you create a powerful synergy that boosts your career trajectory.

Now, onto the juicy part—how do you keep growing these skills without feeling like you're just treading water? Continuous learning is key, and thankfully, the world has moved beyond dry, lengthy lectures that make your ADHD mind scream for a distraction. Instead, think about engaging in experiential learning, where you can dive into hands-on projects or simulations that mirror real-world challenges. This type of learning not only keeps you engaged but also allows you to experiment and learn from your mistakes in a dynamic, real-time environment.

Micro-learning sessions can also be a game-changer. These are short, focused segments of learning designed to fit easily into your day without overwhelming your brain. Imagine learning a new software program through quick, five-minute tutorials instead of a marathon session that leaves you frazzled. And don't overlook the power of interactive educational tools, which can transform a mundane learning task into an engaging, and even fun, activity. Tools like virtual reality simulations or interactive webinars that allow you to participate actively can enhance your learning experience, making the information stick better and longer.

But here comes the tricky part—how do you keep the fire of motivation burning long after the initial spark of enthusiasm has dimmed? First, remember that learning is more fun with friends. Joining study groups or online forums can not only provide support but also deepen your understanding as you exchange ideas and experiences. Setting up learning challenges, like mastering a new skill every quarter, can also provide a structured yet exciting pathway to growth. And let's not forget about integrating your personal interests with skill development. Love gaming? How about learning to code by creating your own game? Passionate about music? Maybe dive into sound engineering or learn how digital marketing can help promote your music projects.

To wrap up, here are some ADHD-friendly resources to get you started. Look for mentorship programs that match you with industry professionals who understand the highs and lows of navigating a career with ADHD. Industry conferences that offer workshops in innovative formats and specialized training sessions designed for different learning styles can also be invaluable. These resources are not just stepping stones in your skill development journey—they are bridges to new opportunities, expanded networks, and a deeper understanding of how you can turn your ADHD challenges into your greatest career assets.

12.3 Preparing for Career Transitions

Imagine this scenario: You're sitting at your desk, staring at the same old tasks, feeling the tickle of restlessness creeping up your spine. Your coffee doesn't taste as good as it used to, and the projects that once sparked excitement now ignite only a flicker. These, my friend, might be the whispering winds of change, signaling it might be time for a career transition. Recognizing these signs isn't just about acknowledging that you're bored or burned out; it's about understanding how these feelings align with ADHD tendencies like seeking new stimuli and needing diverse challenges to stay engaged.

The first sign to watch for is burnout, which isn't just about feeling tired. It's the emotional and physical exhaustion that comes from prolonged stress, where your job feels less like a challenge and more like a chore. Then there's the lack of advancement opportunities. If you've been stuck in the same position with no sight of upward movement, despite your best efforts and creative input, it's a signal that the environment might not be right for your growth. Decreasing job satisfaction can also creep in subtly. It starts with the Sunday scaries—that dread of Monday mornings—which then seeps into the rest of your week. These symptoms are particularly poignant for professionals with ADHD, who thrive on passion and engagement to channel our energies productively.

Once you recognize these signs, the next step is not just to leap into the unknown but to plan meticulously. Planning for a career transition involves several layers, starting with financial planning. Ensure you have a financial cushion that allows you to explore opportunities without panic. This means budget adjustments, perhaps tightening some belts here and there, or even finding temporary gigs during the transition phase. Next is skill alignment, which involves identifying the skills you have and how they transfer to other industries or roles. This might mean taking some short courses or certifications to bridge any gaps. Lastly, don't overlook the power of network leverage. Begin to foster relationships in industries of interest by attending networking events, joining online forums, or even reaching out to contacts who could offer insights or introductions.

Now, let's talk about embracing change as an opportunity. Change can be daunting; it's like standing at the edge of a diving board, where the water below is both inviting and intimidating. But here's where ADHD traits can actually play to your advantage. Your inherent adaptability and creativity are tailor-made for times of transition. These traits allow you to think outside the box, quickly adapt to new environments, and come up with innovative solutions to problems. So, rather than viewing change with trepidation, try to see it as a playground for your ADHD: a place where you can run, jump, and explore all the equipment with the excitement of a kid with a golden ticket.

Support networks during this time are your safety nets. They ensure you don't spiral into self-doubt or isolation. ADHD support groups can be invaluable, offering insights from those who have navigated similar paths and can offer real, tangible advice. Career counselors who specialize in ADHD can provide guidance tailored to your specific ways of processing and responding to change. Additionally, don't underestimate the value of online forums where you can anonymously share your fears, hopes, and experiences, receiving encouragement and advice from peers who understand the nuances of your journey.

In wrapping up this section, remember that preparing for a career transition isn't about reckless jumps or impulsive decisions. It's a thoughtful, well-planned process that considers financial security, aligns your skills with new opportunities, leverages your professional network, and turns ADHD traits into superpowers that propel you into exciting new chapters. As you stand on the brink of this change, remember that each step, each decision, is crafting not just a new career path but a deeper understanding of how your unique brain wiring can thrive in diverse landscapes. Embrace the winds of change with a plan in hand and a network by your side, ready to leap into a future brimming with possibilities.

12.4 Building a Personal Brand with ADHD

Think of your personal brand as your professional fingerprint—unique, identifiable, and leaving a lasting impression wherever it goes. For professionals with ADHD, understanding and shaping this brand is like sculpting our very own superhero persona. It's more than just a buzzword; it's a way of narrating your story, showcasing your strengths, and explaining the unique ways you navigate the world of work.

Why is this crucial? Well, in the bustling marketplace of jobs and opportunities, your personal brand helps you stand out. It's your part of the conversation that happens even when you're not in the room, influencing perceptions and opening doors. For someone with ADHD, your personal brand offers a golden opportunity to control the narrative. Instead of allowing ADHD to be seen as a set of challenges, you can highlight it as a collection of unique strengths. Yes, you might be the person who comes up with ideas at lightning speed, who can pivot between tasks effortlessly, or who uses their hyperfocus to solve complex problems that others wouldn't have the stamina for. These are not just quirks; these are your superpowers.

Crafting this narrative isn't just about patting ourselves on the back. It's about making a strategic impression that resonates across all platforms—be it your LinkedIn profile, your Twitter feed, or your personal blog. Consistency is key here. If you're branding yourself as a creative innovator on LinkedIn but your tweets suggest you dislike change, the mixed messages could confuse potential employers or collaborators. Each platform should be a chapter of the same story, reflecting your strengths and your professional approach consistently.

But here's where it gets really interesting. As someone with ADHD, you know that change is as inevitable as your next big idea. This means that, while consistency is important, so is adaptability. Your personal brand should be a living entity, capable of growth and evolution as you journey through your career. Regularly checking in on your brand's effectiveness is like giving your car a tune-up; it ensures you're still on the fastest route to your destination. Feedback is invaluable here—whether from mentors, peers, or professional branding consultants. They can provide insights that you might be too close to see, helping you tweak your brand to better showcase your evolving skills and goals.

So, as you craft your personal brand, remember to weave your ADHD traits into the narrative in a positive way. Embrace the dynamic creativity, the rapid problem-solving abilities, and the relentless energy that come with ADHD. Let these traits shine across all your professional platforms, creating a cohesive and compelling picture of who you are in the professional world. Monitor and adapt your brand as needed, using feedback to refine and enhance your presence. By doing so, you're not just building a brand; you're opening a window for others to see the true potential of what it means to be a professional thriving with ADHD.

To wrap up, your personal brand is much more than a tool for career advancement. It's a reflection of your unique approach to professional challenges, a badge of honor that showcases your strengths, and a beacon that attracts like-minded professionals and opportunities. Keep it consistent, make it dynamic, and let it evolve as you advance in your career. As we turn the page from personal branding to the next chapter, remember that each step in refining your brand is a step towards crafting a more authentic and impactful professional identity.

Key Takeaways

12.1 Setting Career Goals with ADHD

- **Understanding Achievable Goals**: Use the SMART (Specific, Measurable, Achievable, Relevant, Time-bound) criteria and make goals exciting to maintain interest. Example: "Introduce one innovative sales strategy per month that taps into emerging market trends."
- **Long-Term vs. Short-Term Goals**: Balance between long-term aspirations and engaging short-term goals to maintain motivation. Example: If your long-term goal is to become a department head, a short-term goal might be to lead a small project team successfully.
- **Incorporating Flexibility**: Set adjustable timelines and have contingency plans. Allow room for interest and passion shifts without feeling like starting over.
- **Goal-Setting Workshops and Tools**: Engage in workshops or online courses and use tools like Trello or Asana for tracking goals visually.

12.2 Long-Term Skill Development Strategies

- **Identifying Key Skills**: Understand how ADHD traits intersect with skills needed in your field. Example: Quick decision-making and innovative solutions as strengths.
- **Continuous Learning**: Engage in experiential learning, micro-learning sessions, and interactive educational tools for better engagement and retention.
- **Maintaining Motivation**: Join study groups, set learning challenges, and integrate personal interests with skill development. Example: Learning to code by creating a game if you're passionate about gaming.
- **ADHD-Friendly Resources**: Seek mentorship programs, industry conferences, and specialized training sessions to enhance skills.

12.3 Preparing for Career Transitions

- **Recognizing Signs for Change**: Identify signs like burnout, lack of advancement opportunities, and decreasing job satisfaction.

- **Planning for Transitions**: Ensure financial security, align skills with new opportunities, and leverage your professional network.
- **Embracing Change as Opportunity**: Use ADHD traits like adaptability and creativity to navigate transitions and view change as a playground for growth.
- **Support Networks**: Utilize ADHD support groups, career counselors, and online forums for guidance and encouragement.

12.4 Building a Personal Brand with ADHD

- **Importance of Personal Brand**: A strong personal brand helps you stand out and control the narrative around your ADHD traits.
- **Crafting Your Narrative**: Highlight your ADHD strengths, such as rapid problem-solving and innovative thinking, across all professional platforms.
- **Consistency and Adaptability**: Ensure your brand is consistent across platforms and adaptable to reflect your evolving skills and goals.

- **Feedback and Refinement**: Regularly check in on your brand's effectiveness and use feedback to refine and enhance your professional presence.

Reflection on Building Your Career with ADHD

- **Tailoring the Process**: Customize goal-setting, skill development, career transitions, and personal branding to fit your ADHD traits.
- **Leveraging ADHD Strengths**: Turn ADHD traits into superpowers that propel you forward in your career.
- **Strategic Planning**: Use structured planning, continuous learning, adaptability, and feedback to navigate and excel in your professional journey.

Conclusion

Wow, what a ride it's been! From the first page to this final chapter, we've traveled together through the twists and turns of ADHD in the professional world. We started this journey looking at ADHD through a lens that many might call limiting, but look at us now—seeing it as a beacon of creativity, resilience, and downright innovation. Who would've thought that what often feels like a personal raincloud could actually be our own unique superpower in the workplace?

Throughout our chapters, we've unpacked a toolbox of strategies designed not just to cope but to thrive. From crafting ADHD-friendly time management systems that don't just work, but work wonders, to organizing techniques that turn chaos into a well-oiled machine. We've dove into engagement techniques that make meetings less of a snooze fest, explored stress and anxiety management that can feel like a soothing balm, and celebrated the ADHD strengths that make us stand out stars in the corporate galaxy.

But beyond all these tactics and tools, there's something even more crucial—embracing who you are. ADHD isn't a roadblock; it's a different route on the map of professional life, one that can take us to incredible views not seen on the usual path. It's about turning self-acceptance into a launching pad for continuous growth and seeing every day as a new opportunity to refine, improve, and innovate.

And let's not forget the power of community. None of us is an island, especially not in the ADHD archipelago. Whether online or in the flesh, finding your tribe—others who share these quirks and qualities—can make all the difference. They're not just support; they're proof that the path you're on has been traveled by many others, each with their own stories of struggle and success.

So, what's next for you? This isn't just the end of a book; it's the beginning of what I hope will be an exhilarating chapter in your career. Take these strategies, tweak them, test them, and transform them into something that fits your unique mold. Set those goals, reach out for new learning opportunities, and keep adapting your approach as you climb higher and dive deeper.

Imagine a world where the professional landscape buzzes with the energy of ADHD superpowers fully unleashed. Where creativity, rapid problem-solving, and vibrant innovation are the norms rather than the exceptions. You are an integral part of this vision. By embracing your ADHD in your professional life, advocating for neurodiversity, and sharing your journey, you help paint a broader, more inclusive picture of success.

Before we part ways, remember this: Your path might have more twists and turns than most, but it's yours to claim, and it's lined with unexpected treasures. Approach each day with curiosity, resilience, and an open heart. The challenges? They're just undiscovered opportunities waiting for you to tap into.

I'd love to keep this conversation going. Share your stories, insights, or even the occasional rant about a particularly chaotic day. Connect with me on social media, drop me an email, or swing by my website. Let's keep building this community, one shared experience at a time.

Here's to you, the real-life superheroes with ADHD. May your careers be as vibrant and dynamic as you are. And never forget: In the grand story of your life, you're the hero. Let's make it an epic one.

Cheers to new beginnings and uncharted territories!

Phoenix J. Waldren

To My Beloved Family,

From the depths of my heart, I extend my sincerest gratitude to each one of you for the unwavering strength, patience, support, and love you've shown me through our many travels around the world. Our journey together, marked by obstacles and challenges, has been the foundation upon which I've built my dreams. Your steadfast belief in my abilities, even when faced with adversity, has been the cornerstone of my journey to write a book that aspires to touch and improve lives. In moments of doubt, it was your conviction that rekindled my resolve and inspired me to press forward. Your encouragement has been my guiding light, illuminating the path when the road seemed daunting and the nights endless. Without you, this dream would not have been possible. I love you to infinity.

I am profoundly thankful to the Heavenly Father for His countless blessings. It is through His grace that I have been molded into the person I am today, equipped with the determination and spirit to embark on this meaningful endeavor. The journey of writing this book has been more than a pursuit of a personal dream; it has been a testament to the power of faith, the beauty of shared hopes, and the strength

derived from a family's love.

To say 'thank you' feels inadequate to express the depth of my gratitude. Yet, these words carry the weight of my appreciation and recognition of your invaluable contribution to my life and this project. I am immensely grateful for your sacrifices, your unwavering support, and the endless love you've bestowed upon me. Together, we have sown the seeds for a legacy that, God willing, will flourish and extend its reach far beyond our imaginations.

With all my love and deepest thanks,

Phoenix J. Waldren

Keeping the Game Alive

Now that you have everything you need to comprehend, dominate, and excel in your career, it's time to pass on your newfound knowledge and show other readers where they can find the same help.

Simply by leaving your honest opinion of this book on Amazon, you'll show other ADHD professionals where they can find the information they're looking for, and pass their passion for achieving career success forward.

Thank you for your help. The community of Professionals with ADHD is kept alive when we pass on our knowledge – and you're helping me to do just that.

Scan the QR code

References

- ADDitude. (n.d.). 15 best assistive learning tools for students with ADHD. ADDitude. *https://www.additudemag.com/assistive-technology-education-applications-adhd-students/*

- ADDitude. (n.d.). 6 secrets to goal setting with ADHD. ADDitude. *https://www.additudemag.com/achieving-personal-goals-adhd/*

- ADDitude. (n.d.). ADHD adults: Building a network of friends. ADDitude. *https://www.additudemag.com/building-your-network-of-friends/*

- ADDitude. (n.d.). ADHD success stories: 6 superstars with attention deficit. ADDitude. *https://www.additudemag.com/adhd-success-stories-6-superstars-with-attention-deficit/*

- ADDitude. (n.d.). Born this way: Personal stories of life with ADHD. ADDitude. *https://www.additudemag.com/adhd-personal-stories-real-life-people-living-with-adhd/*

- ADDitude. (n.d.). Entrepreneurship and ADHD: Fast brain, fast company? ADDitude.
https://www.additudemag.com/entrepreneurship-adhd-business-research-traits-stories/

- ADDitude. (n.d.). Evernote: Best note-taking app for college freshmen. ADDitude.
https://www.additudemag.com/evernote-best-note-taking-app-adhd-college-freshman/

- ADDitude. (n.d.). How ADHD warps time perception. ADDitude.
https://www.additudemag.com/wasting-time-adhd-and-time-perception/

- ADDitude. (n.d.). How to practice mindfulness with ADHD: Meditation for adults. ADDitude.
https://www.additudemag.com/how-to-practice-mindfulness-adhd/

- ADDitude. (n.d.). Mindfulness meditation: ADHD symptom relief with breath. ADDitude.
https://www.additudemag.com/mindfulness-meditation-for-adhd/

- ADDitude. (n.d.). Straightforward ADHD tools and technology for adults. ADDitude.
https://www.additudemag.com/adhd-tools-technology-for-adults/

- ADDitude. (n.d.). *The science of reward and punishment. ADDitude.* https://www.additudemag.com/positive-reinforcement-reward-and-punishment-adhd/

- ADDitude. (n.d.). *Time management skills for ADHD brains: Practical advice. ADDitude.* https://www.additudemag.com/time-management-skills-adhd-brain/

- ADDitude. (n.d.). *Your rights to ADHD accommodations at work. ADDitude.* https://www.additudemag.com/adhd-law-americans-with-disabilities-act/

- Bariso, J. (2020, October 20). *Emotionally intelligent people embrace the 5-minute rule. Inc.* https://www.inc.com/justin-bariso/emotionally-intelligent-people-embrace-5-minute-rule.html

- Beyond BookSmart. (2021, June 29). *ADHD and emotional dysregulation: Signs & how to improve. Beyond BookSmart.* https://www.beyondbooksmart.com/executive-functioning-strategies-blog/adhd-emotional-dysregulation

- Buffett, W. (n.d.). *Quotes.* Retrieved from BrainyQuote

- Carnegie, D. (1998). *How to Win Friends and Influence People.* Gallery.

- CHADD. (n.d.). ADHD benefits in the workplace. CHADD. https://chadd.org/adhd-weekly/adhd-benefits-in-the-workplace/

- Clockify. (n.d.). How to declutter your digital space. Clockify. https://clockify.me/blog/managing-time/digital-declutter/

- Ckacz Education. (2020, June 2). Visual aids: A vital tool for students with ADHD. Medium. https://medium.com/@ckaczeducation/visual-aids-a-vital-tool-for-students-with-adhd-bbf3a9eb5b25

- Day Optimizer. (n.d.). Mastering time blocking for ADHD: Your ultimate guide to better focus. Day Optimizer. https://dayoptimizer.com/adhd/mastering-time-blocking-for-ADHD-your-ultimate-guide-to-better-focus/

- Edge Foundation. (2019, November 5). ADHD and the neuroplastic brain. Edge Foundation. https://edgefoundation.org/adhd-and-the-neuroplastic-brain/

- Enna. (2021, May 19). How an ADHD'er can network effectively for success. Enna. https://enna.org/how-an-adhder-can-network-effectively-for-success/

- Ersling, T. (2020, April 6). How I overcame ADHD and became a productivity powerhouse. Medium.

https://medium.com/@troyerstling/how-i-overcame-adhd-and-became-a-productivity-powerhouse-bf6d4a3dfb51

- Healthline. (n.d.). ADHD and multitasking: Challenges and tips for greater success. Healthline.
https://www.healthline.com/health/adhd/adhd-multitasking#:~:text=Still%2C%20adults%20with%20ADHD%20reported,for%20frequent%20switching%20or%20monitoring.

- HSMH. (2021, July 30). Work-life balance strategies for adults with ADHD. HSMH.
https://www.hsmh.co.uk/blog-posts/work-life-balance-strategies-adults-adhd#:~:text=Time%20Management%20Techniques%20for%20Adults%20with%20ADHD&text=Prioritisation%3A%20Break%20down%20tasks%20into,vital%20assignments%20or%20eceive%20due%20attention.

- I'm Busy Being Awesome. (n.d.). How to be a better listener for adults with ADHD. I'm Busy Being Awesome.
https://imbusybeingawesome.com/be-a-better-listener-adhd/

- Jobs, S. (2005, June 12). Commencement address at Stanford University. Stanford Report. Retrieved from
https://news.stanford.edu/2005/06/14/jobs-061505/

- Jordan, M. (1994). I can't accept not trying: Michael Jordan on the pursuit of excellence. HarperCollins.
- Medical News Today. (2020, September 28). Tips for improving organization with ADHD. Medical News Today. https://www.medicalnewstoday.com/articles/adhd-and-organization
- Medscape. (2005, December 7). Functional roles of norepinephrine and dopamine in ADHD. Medscape. https://www.medscape.org/viewarticle/523887
- Musk, E. (2017). Elon Musk: Tesla, SpaceX, and the Quest for a Fantastic Future. Ecco.
- National Center for Biotechnology Information. (2010, December 15). The neurobiological basis of ADHD. PubMed Central. https://www.ncbi.nlm.nih.gov/pmc/articles/PMC3016271/
- National Center for Biotechnology Information. (2011, April). Multitasking in adults with ADHD. PubMed. https://pubmed.ncbi.nlm.nih.gov/21461781/
- National Center for Biotechnology Information. (2019, July). Social skills training for attention deficit hyperactivity disorder (ADHD). PubMed Central. https://www.ncbi.nlm.nih.gov/pmc/articles/PMC6587063/
- Not Neurotypical Blog. (2017, January 12). Small and discreet fidget toys. Not Neurotypical Blog.

https://notneurotypicalblog.wordpress.com/2017/01/12/small-and-discreet-fidget-toys/

- Nivati. (2022, March 14). *12 best workplace stress relief techniques for the office*. Nivati.

https://www.nivati.com/blog/12-best-workplace-stress-relief-tips-techniques

- Ochsner, K. N., & Gross, J. J. (2008). *Cognitive strategies to regulate emotions—current evidence and future directions*. Frontiers in Psychology, 2, 275.

https://www.ncbi.nlm.nih.gov/pmc/articles/PMC3887268/

- PsychCentral. (2020, November 2). *Time management and ADHD: Tips for success*. PsychCentral.

https://psychcentral.com/adhd/time-management-tips-for-people-with-adhd

- Psychology Today. (2021, June 15). *6 ways to combat procrastination for adults with ADHD*. Psychology Today.

https://www.psychologytoday.com/us/blog/the-best-strategies-for-managing-adult-adhd/202106/6-ways-to-combat-procrastination-for-adults

- Sehgal, N. (2021). *Effect of environmental clutter on attention performance in adults with ADHD*. Journal of Environmental Psychology, 74, 101489.

https://www.sciencedirect.com/science/article/pii/S2211364921000701

- Self. (2020, October 12). Hiring a coach for my ADHD transformed my life. Self.
https://www.self.com/story/hiring-adhd-coach-transformed-my-life

- Shapiro, S. (2019, August 22). Best teaching practices and adult ADHD: 5 highly effective strategies for the classroom & work environment. Scott Shapiro, MD.
https://www.scottshapiromd.com/best-teaching-practices-and-adult-adhd-5-highly-effective-strategies-for-the-classroom-work-environment/

- Strive. (2023, December 22). 75 Best Eric Thomas Quotes For Motivation - The STRIVE. The STRIVE.
https://thestrive.co/motivational-eric-thomas-quotes/

- The ADHD Centre. (2020, September 25). Succeeding in the workplace with ADHD: Strategies for young professionals. The ADHD Centre.
https://www.adhdcentre.co.uk/succeeding-in-the-workplace-with-adhd-strategies-for-young-professionals/

- Wise Squirrels. (n.d.). Mastering meetings with ADHD: Strategies for success in-person and online. Wise Squirrels.
https://wisesquirrels.com/articles/mastering-meetings-with-adhd-strategies-for-success-in-person-and-online

- Zapier. (2020, August 25). 3 to-do list apps that actually work with ADHD. Zapier. https://zapier.com/blog/adhd-to-do-list/

- A quote by Benjamin Franklin. (n.d.). https://www.goodreads.com/quotes/23590-do-not-anticipate-trouble-or-worry-about-what-may-never

- Joshua Becker Quotes (Author of The More of Less). (n.d.). https://www.goodreads.com/author/quotes/4397208.Joshua_Becker

- WWDC Closing Chat | all about Steve Jobs.com. (n.d.). https://allaboutstevejobs.com/videos/misc/wwdc_1997_closing_chat

Made in the USA
Las Vegas, NV
26 March 2025